DESERTS

edited and with an introduction by
WAYNE GRADY

DESERTS

A LITERARY COMPANION

 David Suzuki Foundation

GREYSTONE BOOKS
DOUGLAS & MCINTYRE PUBLISHING GROUP
VANCOUVER/TORONTO/BERKELEY

Greystone Books
A division of Douglas & McIntyre Ltd.
2323 Quebec Street, Suite 201
Vancouver BC Canada V5T 4S7
www.greystonebooks.com

David Suzuki Foundation
219–2211 West 4th Avenue
Vancouver BC Canada V6K 4S2

Library and Archives Canada Cataloguing in Publication
Deserts : a literary companion / edited and with an introduction by
Wayne Grady; series editor Wayne Grady. (Greystone natural wonders series).
Co-published by the David Suzuki Foundation.

ISBN 978-1-55365-326-4

1. Deserts—Literary collections. I. Grady, Wayne
PN6071.D44D48 2008   808.8'032154   C2007-907246-1

Jacket and text design by Peter Cocking
Jacket photo by G. Lekegian/Getty Images
Printed and bound in Canada by Friesens
Printed on acid-free paper that is forest friendly (100% post-consumer
recycled paper) and has been processed chlorine free.
Distributed in the U.S. by Publishers Group West

We gratefully acknowledge the financial support of the Canada Council for the
Arts, the British Columbia Arts Council, the Province of British Columbia through
the Book Publishing Tax Credit, and the Government of Canada through the Book
Publishing Industry Development Program (BPIDP) for our publishing activities.

CONTENTS

INTRODUCTION

SINCE DESERTS ARE generally associated with a paucity of water, the consummate desert species must be the kangaroo rat. It never drinks, but manufactures its own water internally, out of hydrogen and oxygen absorbed by its cells from what it eats. We humans have to look to external sources for our water, and so we tend to avoid deserts. The American geographer Peveril Meigs defined "desert" as any region that receives less than 25 centimeters of rainfall annually, but there are parts of Chile and the Sahara that have not been rained on for decades. There are other deserts in which more people have drowned in rain-swollen wadis than have died from dehydration.

To those unfamiliar with them, deserts are places that have been deserted, abandoned; they are uninhabited and uninhabitable wildernesses in which nothing lives. The English poet Thomas Hood thought there were three locations in the world

9

where absolute silence reigned: "In the cold grave—under the deep deep sea / Or in the wide desert where no life is found."

As the kangaroo rat proves, however, Hood was wrong about deserts, for they are neither silent nor lifeless. Although they can appear to be alien ground, they may simply be speaking to us in an ancient language. "To those who listen," writes Joseph Wood Krutch in *The Voice of the Desert*, "the desert speaks of things with an emphasis quite different from that of the shore, the mountains, the valleys or the plains." For one thing, he says, the desert is conservative rather than radical; it exhorts us to husband our energies rather than to spend them profligately, as does a tropical rainforest. "The heroism which it encourages is the heroism of endurance, not that of conquest."

Because deserts are dry, they are also hot during the day and cold at night. The lack of cloud cover allows 95 percent of the sun's radiation to strike the exposed ground (compared to the 1 percent that reaches the floor of a tropical forest); after dark, 95 percent of the heat generated during the day dissipates. Deserts can remain dry even during rainstorms. In the Gobi Desert, where the temperature at the pebbly surface sometimes reaches 150°F, I experienced what is known as "ghost rain," rain that fell when the sand was so hot the water evaporated before it hit the ground. My head was soaked; my feet remained dry. And yet I was continually amazed by the variety and tenacity of the creatures and plants that managed to live there.

Far from being deserted, deserts are among the most diversely populated habitats on the planet. As Krutch notes, the heat and drought experienced in the desert are no more difficult to tolerate, for some animals, than the long, cold, wet winters of the north. Adaptation simply takes different forms. Our kangaroo rat, a nocturnal rodent of the American southwest that is neither rat nor mouse, can leap up to ten feet when pursued by a predator such as a coyote or a great horned owl. The kangaroo rat of the Australian desert is a different animal altogether, not a rodent but a marsupial. Other animals, such as bobcats, rabbits, mountain sheep, gophers, and prairie dogs, call the desert home. As do plants, some with long tap roots that penetrate six feet below the ground, others with roots that spread out beneath the surface like cups to catch the desert's very occasional rains. Ann Zwinger, in her wonderful book *Wind in the Rock,* excerpted here, includes her own drawings of many plants from the Mojave and Great Basin deserts, including buffaloberry, wallflower, bladderpod, columbine, pennyroyal, mule-ears, and whitemargin gentian. The New Mexico writer John Nichols, in his essay "The Holiness of Water" (also included here), watches dozens of species of amphibians, crustaceans, and insects, from spadefoot toads to fairy shrimp to mosquitoes, emerge from a seemingly dry pond bed after a rain: in the desert, he writes, "water is like coffee, cocaine, crystal meth: it makes everything *alert.*"

In alertness is salvation. If deserts reward conservatism, they also demand the stamina to overcome unendingly harsh conditions. Many writers comment on a desert's ability to turn a person inwards, to send the desert dweller into the cool depths of the self for the resources necessary for survival. Perhaps, as T.E. Lawrence has suggested, that explains why many of the world's major monotheistic religions—Judaism, Christianity, Islam—are desert religions, rising from the vast sand deserts of northern Africa and the Arabian peninsula. Krutch remarks that there is a mystique in the desert, an imparted sense of the puniness of humanity in the face of such overwhelming and indifferent nature. "As a whole the desert is, in the original sense of the word, 'awful.'" Muhammad was born in the desert. Moses led the Israelites across "a terrible wilderness, wherein were fiery serpents and scorpions, and drought, where there was no water." And like a Navajo shaman, Christ was taken into the desert for forty days and forty nights to be tested. The Japanese word for desert, *sabaku,* is also the word for judge.

The desert areas represented in this volume—the Sahara; the Gobi and Taklamakan deserts of China; the four desert regions of Mexico and the American southwest; Australia's Victoria Desert; and the Atacama Desert of Chile—occupy nearly thirty percent of the Earth's continental surface and have filled a great many minds with dread. Three-quarters of Australia is desert: Sydney Upton refers to it as the continent's "dead heart." The subtropical Sahara Desert, with its 3.5-million square miles of wind-blown sand and rock ridges, has become synonymous with our idea of what a desert is. The very name "Arabia" comes from the Hebrew word for desert, *arabah,* which refers to the area surrounding the Dead Sea. Taklamakan, the remotest region of the Gobi Desert, means: "You enter and do not return." The Gobi itself stretches across the entire northern portion of China, separating it from Russia and Mongolia: Colin Thubron, in a passage included here from his book *Behind the Wall*, calls it "the drowner of cities," and Mildred Cable, who spent most of her adult life in China, notes that "with all his ingenuity, man had not been able to hold his own against the all-devouring sands."

And so the desert—any desert—becomes a challenge to humanity's hubris, to our notion that wilderness is something that can be dominated and controlled by us. A desert disproves that notion, and so is a welcome corrective to overweening ambition. A desert is a presence, but it is also an absence, in the sense that it is most often defined by what it is not. In reading these pages, notice how often the contributors write about water, or vanishing species, or existence so reduced to bare essentials that scientists, by studying desert species, are able to come to some idea of life's minimum requirements.

In the American southwest, standing at the southern rim of the Grand Canyon and gazing down at the thin trickle of water that is the Colorado River flowing a mile below the surface of the Arizona desert, I have been struck by the thought that what amazes about the Grand Canyon is not so much what is there— for really, all that is there is air—as what is not there: the billions of tons of desert sand and rock that have been carved off and carried away by eons of moving water. And now even that water has been so diminished by dams and irrigation withdrawals and evaporation that the Colorado no longer reaches the sea.

But if the calm of the desert, as Bruce Berger writes, "is not the calm of infinity but a precise, carved absence, full of hard objects," it is also the emptiness that lies between and feeds living things. The desert is where we go in retreat from the civilized world; it is a harsh wilderness, but perhaps that is why it is still wilderness. It is the last place on earth where, stripped of our social and technological buffers, confronted like Lear's poor, bare, forked animal with elemental nature, we must simply, fundamentally, and absolutely endure.

WAYNE GRADY

PORT ETIENNE

———

ANTOINE DE SAINT-EXUPÉRY

Born in Lyons, France, in 1900, Antoine de Saint-Exupéry did his military service in 1921, training as a pilot, and moved to Paris the next year to concentrate on writing. His first story, *L'Aviateur,* appeared in 1926. He then joined Aéropostale, a commercial airline that flew mail over the Sahara. In 1929, he published the novel *Southern Mail* and was named manager of Aéropostale's Cap Juby station in Rio de Oro, Sahara, where he become permanently enamored of the desert. The following year he moved to South America to fly mail over the Andes, an experience he described in *Night Flight* (1931). In 1939, he wrote *Wind, Sand and Stars,* his memoir of desert flying, excerpted here, and during the Second World War joined the French Army, serving in North Africa as a pilot. His most famous book, *Le Petit Prince,* appeared in 1943; a year later, he was shot down, presumably over the Mediterranean, as neither he nor his plane were ever found.

PORT ETIENNE IS situated on the edge of one of the unsub-
dued regions of the Sahara. It is not a town. There is a stock-
ade, a hangar, and a wooden quarters for the French crews. The
desert all round is so unrelieved that despite its feeble military
strength Port Etienne is practically invincible. To attack it
means crossing such a belt of sand and flaming heat that the raz-
zias (as the bands of armed marauders are called) must arrive
exhausted and waterless. And yet, in the memory of man there
has always been, somewhere in the North, a razzia marching on
Port Etienne. Each time that the army captain who served as
commandant of the fort came to drink a cup of tea with us, he
would show us its route on the map the way a man might tell the
legend of a beautiful princess.

But the razzia never arrived. Like a river, it was each time
dried up by the sands, and we called it the phantom razzia. The
cartridges and hand grenades that the government passed out
to us nightly would sleep peacefully in their boxes at the foot
of our beds. Our surest protection was our poverty, our single
enemy silence. Night and day, Lucas, who was chief of the air-
port, would wind his gramophone; and Ravel's *Bolero*, flung up
here so far out of the path of life, would speak to us in a half-lost
language, provoking an aimless melancholy which curiously
resembled thirst.

One evening we had dined at the fort and the commandant
had shown off his garden to us. Someone had sent him from
France, three thousand miles away, a few boxes of real soil, and
out of this soil grew three green leaves which we caressed as

if they had been jewels. The commandant would say of them, "This is my park." And when there arose one of those sandstorms that shriveled everything up, he would move the park down into the cellar.

Our quarters stood about a mile from the fort, and after dinner we walked home in the moonlight. Under the moon the sands were rosy. We were conscious of our destitution, but the sands were rosy. A sentry called out, and the pathos of our world was re-established. The whole of the Sahara lay in fear of our shadows and called for the password, for a razzia was on the march. All the voices of the desert resounded in that sentry's challenge. No longer was the desert an empty prison: a Moorish caravan had magnetized the night.

We might believe ourselves secure; and yet, illness, accident, razzia—how many dangers were afoot! Man inhabits the earth, a target for secret marksmen. The Senegalese sentry was there like a prophet of old to remind us of our destiny. We gave the password, *Français!* and passed before the black angel. Once in quarters, we breathed more freely. With what nobility that threat had endowed us! Oh, distant it still was, and so urgent, deadened by so much sand; but yet the world was no longer the same. Once again this desert had become a sumptuous thing. A razzia that was somewhere on the march, yet never arrived, was the source of its glory.

It was now eleven at night. Lucas came back from the wireless and told me that the plane from Dakar would be in at midnight. All well on board. By ten minutes past midnight the mails would be transferred to my ship and I should take off for the North. I shaved carefully in a cracked mirror. From time to time, a Turkish towel hanging at my throat, I went to the door and looked at the naked sand. The night was fine but the wind was dropping. I went back again to the mirror. I was thoughtful.

A wind that has been running for months and then drops sometimes fouls the entire sky. I got into my harness, snapped my emergency lamps to my belt along with my altimeter and my pencils. I went over to Néri, who was to be my radio operator on this flight. He was shaving too. I said, "Everything all right?" For the moment everything was all right. But I heard something sizzling. It was a dragonfly knocking against the lamp. Why it was I cannot say, but I felt a twinge in my heart.

I went out of doors and looked round. The air was pure. A cliff on the edge of the airdrome stood in profile against the sky as if it were daylight. Over the desert reigned a vast silence as of a house in order. But here were a green butterfly and two dragonflies knocking against my lamp. And again I felt a dull ache which might as easily have been joy as fear but came up from the depths of me, so vague that it could scarcely be said to be there. Someone was calling to me from a great distance. Was it instinct?

Once again I went out. The wind had died down completely. The air was still cool. But I had received a warning. I guessed, I believed I could guess, what I was expecting. Was I right? Neither the sky nor the sand had made the least sign to me, but two dragonflies and a moth had spoken.

I climbed a dune and sat down face to the east. If I was right, the thing would not be long coming. What were they after here, those dragonflies, hundreds of miles from their oases inland? Wreckage thrown up on a strand bears witness to a storm at sea. Even so did these insects declare to me that a sand-storm was on the way, a storm out of the east that had blown them out of their oases.

Solemnly, for it was fraught with danger, the east wind rose. Already its foam had touched me. I was the extreme edge lapped by the wave. Fifty feet behind me no sail would have flapped. Its flame wrapped me round once, only once, in a caress that seemed dead. But I knew, in the seconds that followed, that the Sahara was catching its breath and would send forth a second sigh. And that before three minutes had passed the air-sock of our hangar would be whipped into action. And that before ten minutes had gone by the sand would fill the air. We would shortly be taking off in this conflagration, in this return of the flames from the desert.

But that was not what excited me. What filled me with a barbaric joy was that I had understood a murmured monosyllable of this secret language, had sniffed the air and known what was coming, like one of those primitive men to whom the future is revealed in such faint rustlings; it was that I had been able to read the anger of the desert in the beating wings of a dragonfly.

Translation by Lewis Galantière

'UWEINAT

RALPH A. BAGNOLD

Ralph Bagnold (1896–1990) served with the British Army during the First World War, and was sent to Egypt in 1925 as an officer of the Royal Engineers. While there he and fellow officer Lt. V.C. Holland explored the Egyptian desert in two Model T Fords, which they found ideal for traveling on sand. In 1929, the pair conceived the idea of crossing the Sand Sea, "an immense mass of sand" that stretched west of Cairo into an unknown part of the Sahara, in search of the mythical oasis of Zerzura. That and other adventures are the subject of Bagnold's 1935 book, *Libyan Sands: Travel in a Dead World*, from which this passage is taken. During the Second World War, Bagnold founded the Long Range Desert Group, and his experience in the Sahara influenced Michael Ondaatje's *The English Patient*. In 1939, Bagnold wrote *The Physics of Blown Sand and Desert Dunes*, a text consulted by NASA in the design of vehicles for use on Mars.

WE HAD NO idea what population might be found at 'Uweinat. In 1923 when Hassanein Bey arrived he found the place occupied by 150 of the black non-Arab Guraan people from the mountains that lie on the far western side of the desert.

These people told him they had migrated from their own country when their independence was threatened by the French some years before, first to Kufra along the caravan road from Wadai, and shortly afterwards from there to 'Uweinat, which they found uninhabited. Here, in this lonely mountain, the voluntary exiles settled, far away from interference, under the leadership of their old tribal chief named Herri.

Hassanein in his book has much to say about this man, who had acted as his guide for a while, leading him from 'Uweinat towards his own home land in the south-west where he had left his property and relatives years before. But he refused to visit them again, turning sadly back to 'Uweinat when the desert edge was reached. Hassanein describes him as gentle-mannered and unassuming, with a benign smile, and an unquestioned dignity in his movements. Three years later Prince Kemal el Din found him there with a diminished following, and was greeted as courteously as Hassanein had been.

There would be little for us to fear from these Guraan, by whom motor-cars would be connected with another visit from the bountiful prince, but there was another possibility. It might have rained in the last year or so. If so, the bedouin from Kufra were likely to have come down with their camels to graze them in the mountain valleys. Our reception by them would be very doubtful, for at the best of times they were suspicious and hostile towards Europeans, and just before leaving Egypt we had heard that Kufra had recently been bombed by the Italians.

From a small-scale map made by Kemal el Din's surveyors we found his old camping site at the mouth of the little gorge of Karkur Murr without difficulty. No one was there, though the sand contained footmarks of men and animals. A few straggling acacia trees grew in the dry gritty water bed just outside—the first green living things we had seen for 600 miles, ever since leaving Dalla.

The cars could be got no farther up the gorge, but half a mile beyond in the cool shadow of the rocks, tufts of grass were found in a damp salt-encrusted clay, and from the foot of a tumble of huge boulders which blocked the valley water seeped out, collecting in a tiny brackish pool. From the surroundings it was clear that the place was very dry and that no rain had fallen for several years. The water was barely drinkable and far less in quantity than had been described by Dr. Ball on the prince's visit.

It had been a trying and an anxious morning, with the loss of a third of our transport and the uncertainty of 'Uweinat; we were disappointed too on realising that our last chance of getting to the western side of the Gilf Kebir by a quick run northwards from here was now definitely shattered by the loss of the car; it would be unwise now to travel with two overloaded cars a mile more than was necessary over the rocky country round the mountain. Fords are amazingly similar to one another; one crown-wheel had broken, it was even chances that another would break too before too long, and we had 500 miles of untraversed country to cross to get back to the Nile.

There was real water here though, brackish though it was, and we drank it just for the joy and freedom of being able to drink without stint. Presently, when the party were rested and washed, with fresh clean skins free of accumulated salt and dirt, the prospect was not so bad. Plenty of interest was to be found on foot. Newbold and Shaw, who for some years had been collecting details of desert rock-pictures found in the Sudan, were intent on seeing the pictures which Hassanein had found in a neighbouring valley; so also were Holland and I, for archeology in the right setting never failed to attract us. Shaw too had his botanising to do, and both he and I were seized by a desire to see what there was away up at the top of the great central citadel.

Next morning, leaving the cars in charge of Prendergast and Dwyer, the remainder of the party started a scramble up the gorge towards Hassanein's valley, cautiously at first with automatic pistols ready cocked. Within a mile a flock of half a dozen goats was met, and soon afterwards, around a couple of stunted date palms, a camel skeleton, a dead donkey, some more grass, and lastly two pools of lovely clear water without a taste of salt.

We were cutting across the eastern foot-hills along a rough track, with the huge pink cliffs of the central massif rising on our left. Some miles on, the track began to descend, leading into the flat sandy bed of a dry valley running out north-east from the main heights towards the open plain. On each side low vertical cliffs offered tempting surfaces at which an idle stone-chipping artist might pass away his day while his cattle browsed on the green-stuff in the valley bed. Some plant life remained even now; acacia trees grew in the sand, rooted in a little moisture down below, and dry cucumber-like stalks and leaves had not been very long dead.

Presently the valley widened; here, after a walk of nine miles, the first pictures appeared. At a casual glance they were very ordinary crude chippings about six inches in size, outlining men and animals, carelessly scrawled over the rock walls, mostly on the shady side of the valley. They were very sharp and hardly weathered; in any other country one would say they were a few years old at most.

But when giraffes appeared, and horned cattle or antelope, and men with bows and shields, and later when on the roof of a cave red-and-white paintings were found of steatopygous waspy-waisted figures characteristic of the Bush-men paintings of South Africa, it dawned on one that these pictures were very strange indeed—dating from a long-past climatic age and a former distribution of mankind.

These rock pictures are found in many parts of North Africa, done in many styles, and are believed to vary in date over a great period of time, being the handiwork of many different peoples and races who have come and gone. Some are thought even to belong to paleolithic days ten or twenty thousand years ago. Their collection and classification are still incomplete, but a great deal of work has been done on them by Abbé Breuil and others. The difficulty seems to be that they are very rarely found definitely associated with any other relics by which they can be linked to the existing framework of our knowledge of prehistoric times. One clear distinction between them can, however, be made; that is whether or not the pictures of animals include the camel, which did not arrive in Africa till the Persian invasion in the sixth century B.C. The majority of the pictures contain no camels, though without their aid few of the sites could be reached by natives in modern times without great difficulty owing to lack of water.

On the following day, while the rest of the party went back in the two cars to retrieve a notebook containing all our survey notes that had been accidentally left fifty miles back along our route, Shaw and I climbed the south-eastern bastion of the main mountain in search of plants and anything else of interest that might be found.

It was by no means the flat-topped plateau it had looked from the plain; for the rock was hollowed out by a freak of erosion into spires and pinnacles over a hundred feet in height, separated by winding passages mostly so narrow that only the invisible mountain sheep, whose fresh droppings were to be seen in plenty, could squeeze their way through.

Wandering through this labyrinth, we came out at unexpected places to the threshold, as it were, of a broken doorway high up in the battlements of some ruined castle, with nothing but a sheer thousand-foot drop beneath. From these openings the enormous yellow plain could be seen, featureless and glaring with reflected sunlight, reaching away and away in all directions (except to the south, where the peak of Kissu many miles distant rose like a lone cathedral) to a vague hazy horizon. Once with glasses we caught sight of the two cars hurrying off across the plain—two tiny dots so far away that they hardly seemed to move, although seemingly just down below us, scarcely yet clear of the pimply black foot-hills. Soon they dwindled to nothing and were lost to view at a point still comparatively close to us, with the plain rolling on beyond them to a horizon far up in the sky.

With that little vision came a sudden overwhelming sense of the remoteness of the mountain—as if it included the whole world and was floating by itself, with Kissu peak as its satellite, in a timeless solitude.

At sunrise next morning, while breakfast was cooking and the sleepier members of the party sat up still anchored to their blankets, a man walked quietly out of the gorge towards us, clad in the ragged blue garment of the Guraan.

We had known from fresh footmarks in the rock-picture valley two days before, that the place was still inhabited, but his actual appearance came as rather a shock. Except for the goats he was the first and only animal we saw during a thousand miles of our journey.

He knew a little Arabic, and he and Newbold chatted, squatting together on the ground. He was Herri's personal slave. Herri himself was ten miles away on the other side of the mountain. There had been no rain for several years, and Herri's following had dwindled to six men scattered over 'Uweinat in ones and twos scratching about for some sort of nourishment.

Hassanein had reported that in 1923 the Guraan were living on a kind of flour ground from the boiled seeds of the colocynth or bitter-apple. Shaw came across a dish-shaped grinding stone showing signs of white flour on it which he thought at the time was from some sort of grain, for Kemal el Din in 1925 had seen a crop of grass growing in a mud-pan out on the plain near by. It may, however, have been the colocynth grindings which we saw, though the place seemed now too dry even for that desert creeper.

We gave him a sugar-loaf and some tea, and he plodded slowly back into the gorge. Later we motored round to 'Ain Duwa, the western of the two water pools twenty miles away along the southern face of the mountain, hoping to find one or two of the others if not Herri himself; but it too being deserted, we were forced to leave the presents we had brought on a rock with a note in Arabic saying how sorry we were that he was out when we called. Some months later in Cairo we had the satisfaction of hearing that our visit and letter was such an event that the old gentleman had mounted his camel and ridden straight to Kufra, 200 miles away, to tell them about it.

Since our visit this last remainder of the 'Uweinat Guraan have disappeared; it was a pity that we missed this chance of seeing probably the last permanent inhabitants that 'Uweinat will have for many years to come.

THE CAMEL OF CAIRO

SARA JEANNETTE DUNCAN

Born in Brantford, Canada West, in 1861, Sara Jeannette Duncan became a highly successful journalist, writing editorials for the *Washington Post*, a column for the Toronto *Globe* and serving as parliamentary correspondent for the *Montreal Star*. On a round-the-world tour begun in 1888 with fellow journalist Lily Lewis, she met Everard Cotes, a museum director in Calcutta, married him in 1890, and lived for the next thirty years in India. Although she is best known for her autobiographical novel, *The Imperialist* (1904)—a portrait of staid Brantford—her first book was *A Social Departure: How Orthodocia and I Went Round the World by Ourselves*, published in 1890, from which this account of her stay in Egypt is excerpted. She loved the exotic, and was a witty and intelligent observer of life, as this vivid description of a desert camel in Cairo shows. She wrote several more novels, including *Cousin Cinderella: A Canadian Girl in London* (1908), and spent her last years in England where she died in 1922.

BUT I HAVE not told you of the indescribable din of this street of Cairo; how the carriages dash recklessly—whips cracking—among the people; how the water-sellers clash their brass vessels and cry, "Drink, O Faithful!" and the pedlars of lemons and of lupins, of dates and sweet cakes, call upon Allah to make their baskets light; and the money-changers sit at the corners of the streets endlessly chaffering and clinking, and the donkeys bray, and the people talk in many tongues, and the camel joins the chorus in his own distinctive voice.

Ah, the camel of Cairo! I tremble on the verge of a paragraph about him; I know I cannot do him justice, but the emotions that came from the first one that gladdened us in the Mousky that morning crowd back upon me and will not be dismissed. He was immediately behind us—we turned suddenly and saw him, a great pack of green clover on his back, looking down at us with a bland and level condescension which seemed intended to allay our nervousness, though it had not precisely that effect. We had grown used to the donkeys. They trotted, and obeyed a stick from the rear. When they elbowed us it was with apology, and when we turned to speak to each other and found an asinine countenance close to our own it was always full of deference. They occupied the human plane, moreover; their joys and sorrows were, in a manner, ours; they shared the common lot. And one didn't get out of their way; one kept them waiting.

But this slow, strange beast, with his lofty and deliberate assertion of precedence—we made room for him at once, and without cavil, as he mutely requested us to do, and as he passed we stood and looked at him. We saw that everybody made room for him, as if he were incarnate fate. He went quietly and comfortably through the narrowest lanes and densest crowds by the mere force of his personality. He was the most impressive living thing we saw in Egypt, not excepting two Pashas and a Bey. He was engaged with large philosophies, one could see that, and the superciliousness in the curve of his neck was unavoidable. Ages ago he had tried to make up for it with a smile, a smile of the simple primary sort, acquired before the world learned smiling hatred, a mere pulling up of the corners of the mouth, expressing pure amiability, and from generation to generation the smile had become a fixture, though he gives one the impression that he would dispense with it now if he could. For he thinks and remembers and compares. The people have changed and have divided their inheritance; he is a solitary survival, and has preserved his. Their traditions are his history: he knew the desert world; he walked in the train of the Queen of Sheba; he could retail scandals of the Court of Solomon. And he bends his back to the modern burden, neither more nor less than he carried then, because it is, and has always been, part of the formula of life for him. When they took it off I suppose he was relieved, but he did not show it in any way; when they made it too heavy he simply looked round communicatively and declined to get up.

He did what was required of him with a superior leisurely dignity that was elevating to observe. He never hurried; I did not see him beaten. As to his personal appearance, it is difficult to say that he is beautiful; but I defy you to go to Cairo and thereafter call him ugly. He seems to belong to a world of different standards in these matters. His skin is the most interesting thing about him, to a lover of the antique. It seems to have been in constant use since the original camel took it out of the ark with him, it is so battered and tattered, so seamy and patched, so disreputably parchment-coloured. Orthodocia did not love this Egyptian as I did; she said he was known to have a vicious bite, and his airs were insupportable. "Moreover," she remarked, "I want to see a *new* camel!" But, though we gazed on many clover-laden trains winding through many *sharia* of Cairo, we never saw one that was not indisputably second-hand.

THE CARAVAN MEETS
WITH DISASTER

SVEN HEDIN

Swedish geographer Sven Anders Hedin was born in Stockholm in 1865, and from the day in 1880 when he witnessed the triumphant homecoming of the Finnish explorer Nils Nordenskiöld from the Northeast Passage, he was inspired to pursue risky adventures. Five years later he was working as a tutor on the Caspian Sea, where "the glamour of the whole Orient was to unfold before me." He spent the rest of his life exploring the remotest places on the globe. In 1894, he undertook an expedition into central Asia in search of the lost city of Li Hsieh that, according to Chinese legend, had been buried in the Taklamakan Desert under masses of sand. He found the ruins on the desiccated Chara River delta in 1896 and completed the journey by crossing the Gobi on foot to Peking. Much of his autobiography, *My Life as an Explorer,* published in 1925 and the source of this excerpt, is devoted to this dramatic crossing. Hedin died in Sweden in 1952.

. . .

EARLY IN THE MORNING of April 28, a sandstorm, the like of which we had never seen, broke over our camp. The wind heaped piles of sand on us, on our belongings, and on our camels; and, when we rose, at dawn, to meet another terrible day, we found we were nearly buried in sand. Everything had sand in it. My boots and my cap, my leather instrument-bag, and other articles had disappeared; and we had to dig the things out again with our hands.

There was little actual daybreak to speak of. Even at noon the darkness was more pronounced than at dusk. It was like marching at night. The air was filled with opaque clouds of drift-sand. Only the nearest camel was dimly visible, like a shadow in this otherwise impervious mist. The bronze bells were inaudible, even when quite near. Shouts could not be heard. Only the deafening roar of the storm filled our ears.

With such weather, it was wise for all of us to stick together. To fall behind the caravan, or to let it get out of sight, was to lose it forever. The traces of camels and men were obliterated almost instantly.

The gale grew into a hurricane. The velocity of the wind was fifty-five miles an hour. During the most violent blasts we nearly choked. Sometimes the camels refused to walk, but lay down and stretched their necks along the sand. Then we also threw ourselves down, pressing our faces against their flanks.

One of the younger camels began to stagger during that day's march. He was being led in the rear of the caravan by Yolchi. As I walked along, I kept my hand on one of our boxes, so as not to lose my way. Yolchi came up and shouted in my ear that the camel had fallen on a steep sand-ridge, and could not be induced to get up. At once I ordered a halt, and sent Mohammed

Shah and Kasim to save the camel. They returned in a few minutes and reported that the trail had disappeared, and that they
had been unable to find the camel in the thick clouds of whirling
sand. As it was a question of life and death for all of us, we had
to leave him, as well as his load, consisting of two boxes of provisions, ammunition, and furs. He was doomed to die of thirst
in this suffocating, murderous desert.

In the evening, when we camped, we got rid of the other
boxes, which contained provisions, furs, blankets, rugs, pillows,
books, cooking-apparatus, kerosene, pots and pans, a set of
agate-ware and china, etc. Everything that could be dispensed
with was packed in boxes, which we stowed between two dunes.
Into the crest of the higher dune we drove a pole, to the top of
which we tied a newspaper, to serve as a beacon. We kept only
enough food for a few days. All the liquid tinned food was distributed among the men. They ate it, first satisfying themselves,
however, that it contained no pork. They greedily drank up
the oil in the sardine-tins. Another pack-saddle was emptied of
its hay stuffing; but the camels ate the hay without relish, their
throats were so parched. In the evening, I drank my last cup of
tea. Only two small iron jars of water were now left.

The gale subsided during the night. At sunrise, on the
twenty-ninth of April, Islam reported that one of the water-jugs
had been stolen during the night. Everyone suspected Yolchi,
especially as he did not show up until the next morning.

We started off with the remaining five camels. Again we
made observations from the high dunes. There was only a sea

of yellow sand in all directions. Not a sign of organic life even the size of a pin-head. Yet, to our surprise, we found the grey, porous trunk of a poplar, withered for centuries, perhaps for thousands of years. How many dunes had passed over this tree, dead ever since its roots had ceased to reach the moisture of the subsoil.

As a result of the storm, the air was filled with flying particles of sand, which tended to moderate the sun's heat somewhat. Yet the camels walked slowly, with tired, deliberate steps. The last two bronze bells tinkled in slow, solemn measure. We moved on for twelve and a half hours, with countless stops and interruptions. From our night's camp, nothing could be seen to indicate that the desert sea had a shore.

The next morning, the thirtieth of April, the camels got all the butter that was left. There still remained a few cups of water in the last iron jar. While the camels were being laden, we came upon Yolchi, with the jug to his mouth. Foaming with rage, Islam and Kasim fell upon him, beat his face, threw him to the ground, kicked him, and would have killed him on the spot, had I not intervened.

Hardly one cup of water remained. I told the men that at noon I would dip the corner of a handkerchief in it and moisten my lips and theirs, and that the last drops would suffice for a small mouthful for each. At noon I moistened their lips, but in the evening the jug was empty. I do not know who the guilty one was, and it was no use holding a trial. The desert was endless, and we were all headed toward certain death.

When we had gone along for a while, the dunes became lower, averaging about twenty-five feet. A wagtail was hopping on a dune-comb. Islam Baï was so buoyed up by this, that he begged permission to hurry eastward with the empty iron jugs, and to return after he had filled them at the nearest water. But I would not allow it. He was more necessary to us now than ever.

Yolchi was missing again; and the others were furious. They thought he had deliberately understated the distance, after he had stolen the water from us that night, in the hope that we would die of thirst, and that afterwards he would steal our Chinese silver and find refuge in the woods along the Khotan-daria. But I think their suspicions were groundless.

That night, I wrote what I supposed were to be my last lines in my diary: "Halted on a high dune, where the camels dropped. We examined the east through the field-glasses; mountains of sand in all directions, not a straw, no life. All, men as well as camels, are extremely weak. God help us!"

May Day, a springtime feast of joy and light, at home in Sweden, was for us the heaviest day on our *via dolorosa* through the desert.

The night had been quiet, clear, and cold (36°); but the sun was hardly above the horizon, when it grew warm. The men squeezed the last drops of the rancid oil out of a goat's skin, and gave them to the camels. The day before, I had not had a single drop of water, and the day before that, only two cups. I was suffering from thirst; and when, by chance, I found the bottle in which we kept the Chinese spirits for the Primus stove, I could not resist the temptation of drinking some of it. It was a foolish thing to do; but nevertheless I drank half the bottle. Yoldash heard the gurgling sound, and came toward me, wagging his tail. I let him have a sniff. He snorted, and went away sadly. I threw the bottle away, and the rest of the liquid flowed out into the sand.

That treacherous drink finished me. I tried to rise, but my legs would not support me. The caravan broke camp, but I remained behind. Islam Baï led, compass in hand, going due east. The sun was already burning-hot. My men probably thought I would die where I lay. They went on slowly, like snails. The sound of the bells grew fainter, and finally died away altogether. On every dune-crest the caravan reappeared like a dark spot, smaller and smaller; in every hollow between the dunes, it remained concealed for a while. Finally I saw it no more. But the deep trail, with its dark shadows from the sun, which was still low, reminded me of the danger of my situation. I had not strength enough to follow the others. They had left me. The horrible desert extended in all directions. The sun was burning and blinding, and there was not a breath of air.

Then a horrible thought struck me. What if this was the quiet before a storm? At any moment, then, I might see the black streak, across the horizon in the east, which heralded the approach of a sandstorm. The trail of the caravan would then be obliterated in a few moments, and I would never find my men and camels again, those wrecks of the ships of the desert!

I exerted all my will-power, got up, reeled, fell, crawled for a while along the trail, got up again, dragged myself along, and crawled. One hour passed and then another. From the ridge of a dune, I saw the caravan. It was standing still. The bells had ceased tinkling. By superhuman efforts, I managed to reach it.

Islam stood on a ridge, scanning the eastern horizon, and shading his eyes with his hand. Again he asked permission to hurry eastward with the jugs. But seeing my condition, he quickly abandoned the idea.

Mohammed Shah was lying on his face, sobbingly invoking Allah. Kasim sat in the shadow of a camel, his face covered with his hands. He told me that Mohammed Shah had been raving about water all the way. Yolchi lay on the sand, as if he were dead.

Islam suggested that we continue, and look for a spot of hard clay ground, where we might dig for water. All the camels were lying down. I climbed on the white one. Like the others, he refused to get up. Our plight was desperate. Here we were to die. Mohammed Shah lay babbling, toying with the sand, and raving about water. I realized that we had reached the last act of our desert-drama. But I was not yet ready to give in altogether.

The sun was now glowing like an oven. "When the sun has gone down," I said to Islam, "we will break camp and march all night. Up with the tent!" The camels were freed from their burdens, and lay in the blazing sun all day. Islam and Kasim pitched the tent. I crawled in, undressed completely, and lay down on a blanket, my head pillowed on a sack. Islam, Kasim, Yoldash, and the sheep went into the shade, while Mohammed Shah and Yolchi stayed where they had fallen. The hens were the only ones to keep up their spirits.

This death-camp was the unhappiest I lived through in all my wanderings in Asia.

It was only half-past nine in the morning, and we had hardly traversed three miles. I was absolutely done up, and not able to move a finger. I thought I was dying. I imagined myself already lying in a mortuary chapel. The church-bells had stopped tolling for the funeral. My whole life flew past me like a dream. There were not many hours left me on the threshold of eternity. But most of all, I was tormented by the thought of the anxiety and uncertainty which I would cause my parents and brother and sisters. When I should be reported missing, Consul Petrovsky would make investigations. He would learn that I had left Merket on the tenth of April. All traces after that, however, would then have been swept away; for several storms would have passed over the desert since then. They would wait and wait at home. One year would pass after another. But no news would come, and finally they would cease hoping.

About noon, the slack flaps of the tent began to bulge, and a faint southerly breeze moved over the desert. It blew stronger, and after a couple of hours it was so fresh that I rolled myself up in my blanket.

And now a miracle happened! My debility vanished and my strength returned! If ever I longed for the sunset, it was now. I did not want to die: I *would* not die in this miserable, sandy desert! I could run, walk, crawl on my hands and feet. My men might not survive, but I had to find water!

The sun lay like a red-hot cannon-ball on a dune in the west. I was in the best of condition. I dressed, and ordered Islam and Kasim to prepare for departure. The sunset-glow spread its purple light over the dunes. Mohammed Shah and Yolchi were in the same position as in the morning. The former had already begun his death-struggle; and he never regained consciousness. But the latter woke to life in the cool of the evening. With his hands clenched, he crawled up to me, and cried pitifully: "Water! Give us water, sir! Only a drop of water!" Then he crawled away.

"Is there no liquid here, whatever?" I said.

"Why, the rooster!" So they cut off the rooster's head and drank his blood. But that was only a drop in the bucket. Their eyes fell on the sheep, which had followed us faithfully as a dog, without complaining. Everyone hesitated. It would be murder to kill the sheep to prolong our lives for only one day. But Islam led it away, turned its head toward Mecca, and slashed its carotids. The blood, reddish-brown and ill-smelling, flowed slowly and thickly. It coagulated immediately into a cake, which the men gulped down. I tried it, too; but it was nauseous, and the mucous membrane of my throat was so dry, that it stuck there, and I had to get rid of it quickly.

Mad with thirst, Islam and Yolchi collected camel's urine in a receptacle, mixed it with sugar and vinegar, held their noses, and drank. Kasim and I declined to join in this drinking-bout. The two who had drunk this poison were totally incapacitated. They were overcome with violent cramps and vomiting, and lay writhing and groaning on the sand.

Islam recovered slightly. Before darkness fell, we went over our baggage. I laid everything that was irreplaceable in one pile: notebooks, itineraries, maps, instruments, pencils and paper, arms and ammunition, the Chinese silver (about $1,300), lanterns, candles, a pail, a shovel, provisions for three days, some tobacco, and a few other things. A pocket-Bible was the only book included. Among the things abandoned were the cameras and about a thousand plates, of which about one hundred had already been exposed, the medicine-chest, saddles, clothes, presents intended for the natives, and much besides. I removed a suit of clean clothing from the pile of discarded things, and changed everything, from head to foot; for if I was to die and be buried by the sandstorms in the eternal desert, I would at least be robed in a clean, new shroud.

The things we had decided to take along were packed in soft saddle-bags, and these were fastened to the camels. All the pack-saddles were discarded, as they would only have added unnecessary weight.

Yolchi had crawled into the tent to lie down on my blanket. He looked repulsive, soiled as he was with blood from the lungs of the sheep. I tried to brace him up, and advised him to follow our track during the night. He did not answer. Mohammed Shah was already delirious. In his delirium, he muttered the name of Allah. I tried to make his head comfortable, passing my hand over his burning forehead, begged him to crawl along our trail as far as he could, and told him that we would return to rescue him as soon as we found water.

The two men eventually died in the death-camp, or near it. They were never heard of; and when, after a year had elapsed, they were still missing, I gave a sum of money to their respective widows and children.

All five camels were induced to get up, and they were tied to one another in single file. Islam led, and Kasim brought up the rear. We did not take the two dying men along, because the camels were too weak to carry them; and, indeed, in their deplorable condition, they could not have kept their seats between the humps. We also cherished the hope that we would find water, in which case we were going to fill the two goatskins that we still carried, and hurry back to save the unfortunate ones.

The hens, having satisfied their keen hunger with the dead sheep's blood, had gone to rest. A silence more profound than that of the grave prevailed around the tent. As twilight was about to merge into darkness, the bronze bells sounded for the last time. We headed eastward as usual, avoiding the highest ridges. After a few minutes' walk, I turned about, and gave a farewell-glance at the death-camp. The tent stood out distinctly in the vanishing daylight that still lingered in the west. It was a relief to get away from this ghastly place. It was soon swallowed up by the night.

When it was pitch-dark, I lit the candle in the lantern, and walked ahead, looking for the easiest way. One of the camels collapsed during the march, and lay down immediately, prepared for death, neck and legs stretched out. His bag was placed on "White," the strongest of the four survivors. The dying camel's bronze bell remained with him. Its tinkling was now a thing of the past.

Our progress was desperately slow. Every step was an effort for the camels. Now one, then the other stopped, and had to rest for a while. Islam suffered from fresh attacks of vomiting, and lay writhing on the sand like a worm. In the faint light from the lantern, I lengthened my stride, and went on ahead. I walked thus for two hours. The sound of the bells died away behind me. There was no sound discernible, save the swishing of the sand under my heels.

At eleven o'clock, I struggled up onto a flat, sandy ridge, to listen and to reconnoitre. The Khotan-daria *couldn't* be far away. I scanned the east, hoping to detect the fire of a shepherd's camp; but everything was pitch-dark. Only the stars shone. No sound interrupted the silence. I placed the lantern in a position to serve as a beacon for Islam and Kasim, laid myself on my back, and pondered and listened. My composure, however, remained unshaken.

Far away, the clanging of the last bell again became audible. There were intervals of quiet, but the sound came nearer. After I had waited for what seemed like eternity, the four camels stood forth like phantoms. They came up to me on the ridge and lay down right away. They probably mistook the lantern for a camp-fire. Islam staggered along, threw himself on the sand, and whispered labouredly that he could go no farther. He would die where he was. He made no answer when I tried to encourage him to hold out.

On seeing that the game was up, I decided to forfeit everything except my life. I even sacrificed diaries and records of observations, and took along only what I always carried in my pockets, namely, a compass, a watch, two chronometers, a box of matches, handkerchief, pocket-knife, pencil, a piece of folded paper, and, by the merest chance, ten cigarettes.

Kasim, who still bore up, was happy when I told him to come with me. Hurriedly he took the shovel and pail, but forgot his cap. Later on, he used my handkerchief to protect himself against sunstroke. I bade farewell to Islam, and told him to sacrifice *everything*, but try to save himself by following our track. He looked as if he were going to die, and made no answer.

After a last look at the patient camels, I hurried away from this painful scene, where a man was fighting death, and where the veterans of our erstwhile proud caravan would end their desert-journey for good. I caressed Yoldash, and left it to him to decide whether he would stay or go with us. He stayed, and I never saw the faithful dog again. It was midnight. We had been shipwrecked in the middle of the sea, and were now leaving the sinking ship.

The lantern was still burning beside Islam, but its light soon died out behind us.

Translation by Alfhild Huebsch

THE RUMBLING SANDS

MILDRED CABLE

●　●　●

Mildred Cable, along with Francesca and Eva French, were members of the China Inland Mission, a British organization established to convert the Chinese to Christianity. The "Trio" spent the years 1893 to 1917 in Shanxi Province, then traveled the Silk Road for the next seventeen years, crossing the Gobi Desert five times as itinerant missionaries, wearing Chinese dress, learning local dialects, and enduring many hardships. "Once the spirit of the desert had caught us," Cable wrote, "it lured us on and we became learners in its severe school." They remained in the Gobi until obliged to leave China at the outbreak of the Sino-Japanese War in 1937. This description of the mysterious "Rumbling Sands" is taken from her book of their adventures, *The Gobi Desert* (1944).

●　●　●

THE CONSTANT HURRICANES which sweep the sandy plains have piled up a long line of dunes stretching from Tunhwang away to the Desert of Lob. The range is so long, and the hills are so lofty, and so massed one behind the other, that it seemed incredible such a mighty rampart could be composed wholly of shifting sand. From season to season the contour of the dunes changes, for under the breath of even the lightest breeze the shifting surface runs like sand in an hour-glass, and every wind lifts the clear-cut ridge like spray, though the solid body of the sand-mountain resists the fiercest winter storms.

Behind the great rampart death reigns, and there is not so much sign of life as the track of a passing antelope. Not even a beetle or a lizard would find sustenance in that sterility, yet it was in search of a lake that we first explored the desolate region.

"The skill of man made the Caves of the Thousand Buddhas, but the Hand of God fashioned the Lake of the Crescent Moon," is a popular saying at Tunhwang, and when I asked where to find this Lake of the Crescent Moon, the answer was:

"It lies behind the first range of those sand-hills."

"Is it so very beautiful?" I enquired.

"More beautiful than words can tell," was the answer.

"How far off is the lake?" I asked, remembering the fatigue of toiling through loose sand.

"It is barely four miles from the town, and once there you will find fresh sweet water, a small temple with clean guest-rooms, and a quiet place in which to rest."

This was an encouraging answer, and a few days later we left the city gate with faces turned toward the dunes. Within an hour we were standing at the base of the outermost hill, and where the range was at its lowest we started to climb the steep side, ploughing upwards through sands which buried our feet to the ankle at each step. Near the top, where the slope was almost perpendicular, exhaustion overcame us and every few steps we sank to the ground. All around us we saw tier on tier of lofty sand-hills, giving the lie to our quest, yet when, with a final desperate effort, we hoisted ourselves over the last ridge and looked down on what lay beyond, we saw the lake below, and its beauty was entrancing.

Small, crescent-shaped and sapphire blue, it lay in the narrow space dividing us from the next range like a jewel in folds of warm-tinted sand. On its farther shore stood a small temple surrounded with silvery trees, and on the surface of the lake a flotilla of little black-headed divers were swimming. The downward stretch of the soft slope was an irresistible inducement to slide, and we all came down with a rush, bringing the sand with us like a cataract. Then, for the first time, we experienced the strange sensation of vibrant sands, for as we slid, a loud noise came from the very depths of the hill on which we were, and simultaneously a strange vibration shook the dune as though the strings of some gigantic musical instrument were twanged beneath us. We had, unknowingly, chosen for our slide one of the resonant surfaces of the hill, for, curiously enough, only a few of the dunes are musical and most of them are as silent as they are dead.

The long descent landed us on the edge of the lake and a short distance from the temple door, where the priest received us and led us to a pleasant room in the guests' courtyard.

"You heard the *lui-ing* (thunder-roll) of the hills as you came down," he said. "The sound reached us here, for you chose the right spot to set the sands thundering. Had you been a little farther to east or west, the noise would have been much fainter, and had you come down that farther hill, nothing would have been heard."

"I never knew sands with a 'thunder voice' before," I said.

"You will hear it often while you stay here," was his answer.

This was true, and whenever the wind blew in a certain quarter a roaring came from the dunes. Once, at midnight, we were awakened by a sound like a roll of drums. On that occasion there were brigands in the neighbourhood, and I jumped up in alarm, fearing an attack, but the priest heard me and called out:

"Don't be anxious, Lady. It is only the drum-roll of our sand-hills. Rest your heart."

The old man was quite satisfied to attribute the mysterious noise to the action of the gods whose shrine he tended so carefully, but we were curious to know more about it and began to study the subject. Marco Polo passed this way nearly seven hundred years ago, and he reported desert sand-hills which emitted a sound like distant thunder. These very dunes must have been the "rumbling sands" to which he referred. We also read of "singing sands" in the Arabian desert where Dr. Bertram Thomas and his companions heard a loud noise, which he describes as being like the sound of a ship's siren, coming from some steep sand-hills of which the wind was lifting the crest with a curl like a centurion's helmet. The Arab desert dwellers were familiar with the sound and called that dune "the bellowing sand-hill" because its voice reminded them of the loud bellow of a bull camel. In the Sinai Peninsula, also, travellers have spoken of a locality called "the Hill of the Bell" where a clanging noise is sometimes heard.

The musical sands which are found in these various localities all present special features of dryness and smoothness, for in deserts the transport of sand is effected solely by the wind, and the grains are so constantly rolled to and fro along the ground that each particle becomes smooth, rounded and polished. No such easy explanation, however, is forthcoming by the undoubted fact that one slope "sings" when another, close by, remains silent, and that one course will give a much louder sound than the other. The sands of the Tunhwang dunes are composed of the tiniest fragments of multi-coloured quartz, blue, green, red, purple, grey and white, and this blend of colours gives an iridescent sheen to the sand-hills which responds to every change of light and shade. The sand-girt lake is referred to in many Chinese books as one of the beauty spots of Central Asia, and an envoy sent to Khotan from the Imperial Court in A.D. 938 spoke of its charm and of the towering dunes, which he estimated at five hundred feet in height. A modern explorer quotes this calculation as evidence of the careful, reliable observations made by these early travellers.

JIAYUGUAN

COLIN THUBRON

British travel writer and novelist Colin Thubron was born in London in 1939 and has worked as a filmmaker in Turkey, Japan, and Morocco. His first book, *Mirror to Damascus*, was published in 1967. Since then he has written twenty books, including *Among the Russians* (1983) and *Behind the Wall: A Journey through China* (1987); his novels include *A Cruel Madness* (1984) and most recently *To the Last City* (2002). "My travel books," he writes, "spring from curiosity about worlds which my generation has found threatening... and perhaps from a desire to humanize and understand them." For *Behind the Wall*, Thubron traveled the length and breadth of China, from the Burmese frontier to Hong Kong. In this excerpt he encounters the Gobi's stark landscape at the end of the Great Wall.

. . .

WE REACHED JIAYUGUAN at midday. It was a bungaloid steel town, built for the desert to howl in. I was the only person in my hotel. I gnawed through a near-inedible meal, my head full of the fortress I had glimpsed in the desert close by. In my restaurant the suggestions book had last been inscribed a month before by a lone Japanese: "The service was dreadful. Nobody even spoke to me."

I marched to the fort in cold excitement. It had been rebuilt by the Ming in 1372, and dubbed the "Impregnable Pass under Heaven," and for two millennia, under almost all dynasties, its site had marked the western limit of the Great Wall. From here, since the early years of the Roman Empire, the Silk Road had linked China to the Mediterranean. Even now it invited a journey westward through the Muslim oases of Xinjiang, but the snows and the enormous fort—the traditional terminus of China—dissuaded me.

Massed foursquare on the desert's edge, the slope of its bastions lent it an Assyrian austerity. But as I approached, its ramparts erupted into a delicacy of coloured gate-towers, like a funfair inside a prison, and beyond them a little open-air theater, now restored, had been painted with women and animals in an absurd, defiant sweetness of civilisation at the end of the world.

I climbed its ramparts into the wind, my eyes streaming. To the south, the pass which it defended opened between the black folds of the Mazong range and the white of the Qilian mountains. To the west the Great Wall crossed the desert in isolated scarps and beacon-towers. For a moment, restored to its thirty-foot height, it wrapped the fortress in an outer curtain, then faltered southward a few more miles to its end.

But to the north the Gobi—the drowner of cities—spread void under the colourless sky. A mauve band dissolved its horizon. This was the feared hinterland of the Chinese mind, a chaotic barrenness racked by demons and the ever-lingering nomad. From where I stood, a flying crow, hunting for civilisation, would spread its wings a thousand miles south-west across Qinhai and Tibet before alighting hopelessly on Everest. If instead it endured a thousand miles due west, it would plummet into the wilderness of Taklamakan far short of the Afghan frontier; and northward, after crossing Mongolia, it might wander Siberia for ever.

Into any region beyond the Great Wall, disgraced Chinese were banished in despair. Jiayuguan was "China's Mouth." Those beyond it were "outside the mouth," and its western gate—a vaulted tunnel opening into the unknown—used to be covered with farewell inscriptions in the refined hand of exiled officials. Local people called it the Gate of Sighs. Even if the outcasts survived among the surly Mongols, they would die beyond the reach of any heaven. Demons would torment them in their sandy graves, and Buddhists be condemned to an eternal cycle of barbarian reincarnations.

It was early evening when I started across the sand the last few miles to the Wall's end. I withdrew my head into my overcoat like a tortoise. The wind flayed every chink of exposed skin. In front of me the rampart had long since shed its gloss of tamped clay, and was blistered to earth innards. Often the desert had overwhelmed it, pulling a pelt of stones and camel thorn over the parapets until the sand slid down the far side and sub-sumed them. Ahead, the Qilian ranges were divorced from the plain by haze—a glistening mirage. I could understand why Yu loved them.

I had been walking for two or three miles. The light was fading. The only life was a pair of Bactrian camels browsing on nothing. In the approaching mountains I saw no trace of ram-parts, no sign where the Wall went.

Suddenly the land dropped sheer beneath my feet. In its canyon, two hundred feet deep, wound a concealed river—an ice-blue coldness out of nowhere. It must have started as a gla-cial torrent, but over millennia it had sliced the earth clean. The ground looked so unstable I was afraid to approach the edge. I found myself shivering. All colour had been struck out of it, except for mineral greys and blues. Under the Wall's last, bro-ken tower the river moved to its end in the Gobi through the steel-grey earth under the white mountains.

THE EXPEDITION
TO EUCLA

———

JOHN FORREST

Forrest was born in Bunbury, Western Australia, in 1847. His first expedition to the interior was made at age twenty-two, when he spent five months in an unsuccessful search for the German explorer Ludwig Leichhardt. In 1870, he led an expedition to establish the first overland route from Perth to Adelaide. With six men, including his brother Alexander, he set out first for Esperance, then to Fowler's Bay, and then on to Adelaide, crossing the central deserts of Australia with sixteen horses and scant supplies. He arrived in Adelaide to a hero's welcome; in 1890, he was elected the first premier of Western Australia and was made Baron John Forrest of Bunbury in 1918. That year he fell ill and sailed for England for medical treatment, but died during the voyage. The following report of the first part of his expedition, sent from Port Eucla to the colonial secretary in Perth, is taken from his memoir, *Explorations in Australia*, published in 1875.

PORT EUCLA, 7TH JULY, 1870.

Sir,—It is with much pleasure I have the honour to report, for the information of his excellency the Governor, the safe arrival here of the expedition entrusted to my guidance, as also the meeting of the schooner "Adur."

Leaving Esperance Bay on the 9th of May, we travelled in an easterly direction, over plains generally grassed, to Israelite Bay (situated in latitude 33° 36′ 51″ s., and longitude 123° 48′ E.), which we reached on the 18th May, and met the "Adur," according to instructions issued to the master. Here we recruited our horses and had them re-shod, put the pack-saddles in good order, packed provisions, &c., and gave the master of the "Adur" very strict and detailed instructions to proceed to Eucla Harbour, and await my arrival until the 2nd of September, when, if I did not reach there, he was to bury provisions under the Black Beacon and sail for Fremantle, *via* Israelite and Esperance Bays. Everything being in readiness, on the 30th of May we left Israelite Bay *en route* for Eucla, carrying with us three months' provisions. Keeping near the coast for sixty miles, having taken a flying trip inland on my way, we reached the sand-patches a little to the west of Point Culver, in latitude 32° 55′ 34″ s., and longitude 124° 25′ E., on the 2nd of June.

On the 3rd went on a flying trip to the N.E., returning on the 4th along the cliffs and Point Culver. I found the country entirely destitute of permanent water, but, after leaving the coast a few miles, to be, in places, beautifully grassed. On the coast near the cliffs it was very rocky, and there was neither feed nor water.

Finding there was no chance of permanent water being found, that the only water in the country was in small rocky holes— and those very scarce indeed—and the feed being very bad at Point Culver, I determined, after very mature consideration, to attempt at all hazards to reach the water shown on Mr. Eyre's track in longitude 126° 24′ E., or 140 miles distant.

In accordance with these arrangements, on the 7th day of June started on our journey, carrying over thirty gallons of water on three of our riding horses, and taking it in turns walking. Travelled about N.E. for four days, which brought us to latitude 32° 11′ E., and longitude 125° 37′ E., finding, during that time, in rocky holes, sufficient water to give each horse two gallons. On the fifth day we were more fortunate, and were able to give them each two gallons more, and on the sixth day (the 12th June, Sunday) found a large rock hole containing sufficient to give them five gallons each, which placed us in safety, as the water in longitude 126° 24′ E., was only thirty-two miles distant. Continuing, we reached the water on Tuesday, June 14th, and by observation found it to be in latitude 32° 14′ 50″ S., and longitude 126° 24′ E., the variation of the compass being about 1° 6′ easterly.

The country passed over between Point Culver and longitude 126° 24′ E., was in many places beautifully grassed, level, without the slightest undulation, about 300 feet above the sea, and not very thickly wood. It improves to the northward, being clearer and more grassy, and the horizon to the north, in every place where I could get an extensive view, was as uniform and well-defined as that of the sea. On the route from Point Culver to longitude 126° 24′ E., we were from twenty to twenty-five miles from the sea.

Recruiting ourselves and horses till the 30th, I took a flying trip to the northward. For the first twelve miles from the sea was through a dense and almost impenetrable scrub, when we reached the cliffs, and after ascending them we came into the same description of level country that we travelled over from Point Culver, save that this was more open and grassy, and became still clearer as we proceeded north, until, at our farthest point north, in latitude 31° 33′ S., and longitude 126° 33′ E., scarcely a tree was visible, and vast plains of grass and salt-bush extended as far as the eye could reach in every direction. We found a little water for our horses in rock holes. Returning, we reached camp on June 22nd. On the 23rd we were engaged making preparations for a start for Eucla. In looking round camp, Tommy Windlich found the shoulder-blade of a horse and two small pieces of leather belonging to a pack-saddle. The shoulder-blade is no doubt the remains of the horse Mr. Eyre was obliged to kill for food at this spot.

On June 24th started for Eucla, carrying, as before, over thirty gallons of water, and walking in turns. On the 25th found on the top of the cliffs a large rock hole, containing sufficient water to give the horses as much as they required, and on the 26th were equally fortunate. From the 26th to the 30th we met with scarcely any water, and our horses appeared very distressed, more so as the weather was very warm. On the evening of the 30th, however, we were again fortunate enough to find a water-hole containing sufficient to give them six gallons each, and were again in safety, Eucla water being only thirty miles distant. On the morning of the 1st day of July we reached the cliffs, or Hampton Range (these cliffs recede from the sea in longitude 126° 12′ E., and run along at the average distance of twelve or fifteen miles from the sea until they join it again at Wilson's Bluff, in longitude 129° E. They are very steep and rough, and water may generally be found in rock holes in the gorges. I, however, wished to keep further inland, and therefore did not follow them), and shortly afterwards we beheld the Wilson's Bluff and the Eucla sand-hills. Camped for the night near the Hampton Range, about five miles from Eucla Harbour, and on the 2nd July, on nearing the anchorage, discovered the schooner "Adur" lying safely at anchor, which proved by no means the least pleasing feature to our little band of weary travellers. Camped on west side of Delisser sand-hills, and found water by digging.

The country passed over between longitude 126° 24′ E., as a grazing country, far surpasses anything I have ever seen. There is nothing in the settled portions of Western Australia equal to it, either in extent or quality; but the absence of permanent water is the great drawback, and I do not think water would be procured by sinking, except at great depths, as the country is at least three hundred feet above the sea, and there is nothing to indicate water being within an easy depth from the surface. The country is very level, with scarcely any undulation, and becomes clearer as you proceed northward.

Since leaving Cape Arid I have not seen a gully or water-course of any description—a distance of 400 miles.

The route from longitude 126° 24′ E., to Eucla was generally about thirty miles from the sea.

The natives met with appeared friendly and harmless; they are entirely destitute of clothing, and I think not very numerous.

Very little game exists along the route; a few kangaroos were seen, but no emus—an almost certain sign, I believe, of the scarcity of water.

The health of the party has been excellent; and I cannot speak too highly of the manner in which each member of the expedition has conducted himself, under circumstances often of privation and difficulty.

All our horses are also in splendid condition; and when I reflect how great were the sufferings of the only other Europeans who traversed this route, I cannot but thank Almighty God who has guarded and guided us in safety through such a water-less region, without the loss of even a single horse.

I am afraid I shall not be able to get far inland northward, unless we are favoured with rain. We have not had any rain since the end of April, and on that account our difficulties have been greater than if it had been an ordinary wet season.

I intend despatching the "Adur" for Fremantle to-morrow. The charter-party has been carried out entirely to my satisfaction. With the assistance of the crew of the "Adur" I have repainted the Red and Black Beacons. The latter had been blown down; we, however, re-erected it firmly again. I have also erected a flagstaff, thirty feet high, near camp on west side of Delisser sand-hills, with a copper-plate nailed on it, with its position, my name, and that of the colony engraved on it.

We are now within 140 miles from the nearest Adelaide station. I will write to you as soon as I reach there. It will probably be a month from this date.

Trusting that the foregoing brief account of my proceedings, as leader of the expedition entrusted to my guidance, may meet with the approval of his Excellency the Governor,

I have, &c.,

John Forrest,

Leader of Expedition to Eucla and Adelaide.

THE SAND-RIBBED
DESERT

SYDNEY UPTON

British engineer Sydney Upton conducted his extensive survey of the Australian desert during the 1930s, and published his highly opinionated (and fiercely attacked) book, *Australia's Empty Spaces*, in 1938—one year before the outbreak of the Second World War. Upton declared that the greater part of Australia was "arid and practically useless," that desertification was spreading rapidly, that such largely uninhabited and therefore undefended land was a prime target for foreign invasion, and that Australians should safeguard their homeland by improving communications and developing resources in the interior lowland. However, Upton's own description of the interior was so bleak that it was cited as an argument against a plan to settle 50,000 European Jews in central Australia in 1941. At a time when Australians refused to use the word "desert" to describe their continent, preferring "wilderness" or even "wasteland," Upton's book drew attention to problems facing the country and suggested ways to make the desert more habitable, many of which have since been adopted.

MANY PEOPLE TALK about the golden future before Australia, but rarely does one hear of that slow progressive desiccation to be observed throughout the continent.

There are, as Sir George Wilkins says, parts of Queensland, New South Wales, Victoria, South Australia and Western Australia where the soil is as fertile as any to be found in world-wide travel. In no other continent, however, are natural and agricultural conditions so patchy as they are in the States of Australia. Though there are, of course, many thousands of fertile acres in the great island which, while owned, are as yet unoccupied, there are also many millions of acres which present as little inducement to the settler as do the desolate valleys of the moon.

In good seasons there are hundreds of miles of knee-deep grasses on the flood plains to the east and north of Lake Eyre.

Then the waving grassy plains change to a burning stony desert, the stock cease breeding and gradually die out, the sand drifts over the pitiful fences, and stockyards are no longer used. Yellow, glaring ridges slowly approach and engulf the homesteads. Month after month heavy cloud forms, to clear away again. Intervals of something like ten to twelve years often intervene before the cooling torrents fall, the dry watercourses become swirling maelstroms, and the country waves with grass again.

Large rough spines and a species of acacia called "deadfinish" grow near the edge of Lake Eyre, together with a little salt-bush. Along the dried-up watercourses a thin forest of mulga, box and other indigenous scrub is to be found, the bushes seemingly giant trees in contrast with the tree-less plains.

From Lake Killampurpunna by the Cooper to Bopeechee on the railway to the west of Marree there is one hundred and ten miles of almost completely barren country, the worst in the whole area. The only water is that in the bore-streams—continuously running to waste, precious though it is. For the first fifty miles there are sand-ridges almost meridional in direction about a quarter of a mile apart and of remarkable regularity and straightness. Bushes are to be seen at only quarter-mile intervals.

It is Gregory's "dead heart," a southern extension of the larger waste which lies to the north of Lake Eyre in this region of dismal contrasts. Here, on the one hand, are gibber-strewn expanses upon which no fodder grows, with irregular-shaped rocks ranging from the size of a walnut to that of a water-melon; on the other, a ghastly, treacherous ooze when it rains. Rolling sand and silence, the wine of life and scum-covered brine almost side by side. Little heaps of bones, horrifying in their stillness and the tortures they suggest.

Here Burke and Wills, and maybe Leichhardt and others, were lost, near a land where it is always afternoon. A land apparently unused by the wildest aborigine, nought but parallel and diagonal wavy ribs of red sand, covering an area as big as Ireland, with no sign of life discernible from the air. Only one man, Mr. E.A. Colson, is known to have crossed its surface, from a point on the Finke River about one hundred miles north of Oodnadatta to Birdsville, in May 1936, thus across its southern extremity. All the others who are known to have tried have been driven back or have never returned, being defeated by the series of sand-ribs and the lack of water. It is Taylor's Arunta, or as it is now called, the Simpson Desert, the smaller of the two sandy deserts of the continent.

Lying to the north of Lake Eyre and having an area of some 220 miles by 110 miles, the interior of this land had, as far as is known, never been seen in its completeness until Kingsford Smith flew over it in April 1929.

It was on his return journey to Sydney in the 'plane *Southern Cross*, after having been lost in the Kimberleys, that the famous airman passed over this then unknown area. Amalgamated Wireless at Sydney picked up the following illuminating messages from him on April 25, 1929: "8:32 AM. Melbourne time. We took off from Alice Springs at 8 AM. Our course is now 121 degrees. Speed 78 knots. Altitude 3,000 feet. 9 AM. We are now passing over sandy desert. Altitude 3,200 feet. 9:30 AM. Am still passing over sandy desert. 10 AM. Position of *Southern Cross* is Latitude 25 South, Longitude 136.08 degrees East. Speed 78 knots. Heading for Bourke. 11 AM. We are just passing what was once a lake, but not a drop of water is in it now. Still flying over sandy desert. 12:35. We have now reached the Great Stony Desert. 1 PM. Our position now is Latitude 26·22, Longitude 139·55 East. Course 121 degrees. Speed 77 knots. 2:50 PM. At 1:28 PM we crossed Cooper's Creek. Course 121 degrees. Speed 80 knots."

Never has such an unknown and dreaded area been so blithely crossed and so little attention been paid to the crossing.

From Marree to Birdsville along the well-known track the country today is at its worst. Though there are a number of bores, there is no feed at all. Goyder's Lagoon is a maze of water-courses running in all directions in a black setting of polygonum. Above the lagoon the Diamentina is generally a series of water holes, but it runs for a time almost every year. Its bed is thirty to forty feet below the banks and the water holes are ten to twenty feet deep, full of fish.

The Arunta or Simpson Desert is bounded to the south-east by the Diamentina and Warburton Creeks. From this line sand-ridges run without a break fully two hundred and seventy miles in a North 20° to 40° West direction until they meet the low ranges about ninety miles south-east of Alice Springs. In the main they are in parallel wavy lines, but at intervals the ridges fork and one branch runs diagonally until it meets the next parallel sand-ridge. A quarter to half a mile separates the ridges, from crest to crest, and they are from fifty to one hundred feet high, with gentle slopes on the south-west sides and precipitous faces to the north-east.

For the first hundred miles from the Warburton the spaces between the ridges are stony gibber flats, with scattered clay-pans and a few lines of drainage. The commonest form of vegetation seen is the canegrass-bush (generally dead), which favours the sand-ridges themselves. Spinifex is rare, and mulga and the other acacias are scattered about the claypans and watercourses. Few grasses are to be seen. There are no known eucalypts between the Diamentina and the MacDonnell Ranges, except low boxgum in the Hale River bed.

After a hundred miles the country gets gradually worse, and there are no longer any clay flats or claypans between the sand-ridges, but only drift sand. These conditions prevail for the next hundred miles, which is a dreary waste of sand-ridges, spinifex and mulga. From the air the earth appears a flat pink disk, ribbed from horizon to horizon (thirty to forty miles) by the red sand-ridges and streaked by the darker lines between them where the mulga and spinifex grow closer. Rain, when it falls, sinks straight into the sand, where its life-giving properties are sought by the roots of the hardy plants whose scant foliage braves the scorching air above. From a very low altitude the country looks less desolate. The mulga offers shade; the basins between the sand-ridges look less uninviting; the skyline is broken by the high sand-ridges; yet it is a desert, though one carrying just a little more vegetation of its kind than many of the vast areas in Africa.

In the far north of the Arunta Desert the ridges are less regular than further south, and the vegetation more patchy. Instead of dark streaks between the sand-ridges there are large pink patches of sand almost bare of vegetation, and darker areas of spinifex and mulga, giving a mottled effect like cloud shadows. Here there are many groups of claypans.

Still further north, beyond the sand-ridge desert, the country looks much better, being almost black with vegetation. And yet it was in a country such as this that Anderson and Hitchcock perished of thirst when they had to make a forced landing on their way to join in the search for Kingsford Smith.

The first part of Colson's crossing of this desert, some fifty miles further south than Kingsford Smith's, was over loose, sand-crested hills alternating with limestone flats, in places well vegetated. Beyond this came a stretch of one hundred miles which had a fair amount of desert shrub, and a number of dry salt lakes varying from five miles in length to one and a half in width. The area was then by no means desolate, containing much grass and shrubs, but Colson discounts any possibility of settlement.

Professor Madigan suggested that no more human effort should be expended on the Arunta Desert, but Colson did not find it at all formidable and explorers and police of the Sahara would probably make light of it. Seas of undulating sands have been traversed by motor-car, as well as longitudinal dunes, and even chaotic dunes can now be mastered.

Kingsford Smith spoke of passing what was once a lake, lying in an, as yet, unknown area one hundred miles long and eighty miles across. The Hale and the Todd Rivers once ran into this area, and may do even today, and the Finke with them. Was this lake once another Lake Eyre, or a northern extension of it? Is the whole of this sand-ribbed desert an old lake bed and an example of what may happen to the other dry lakes unless man looks after them?

In days gone by this region was rich in fertility and beauty. Later, numbers of coloured folk traded up and down its rivers, the Cooper and the milk-white-watered Diamentina among them. Even when "White Australia" was young the miles-wide river beds were filled with water instead of sand, and the trails were traversed by thousands of sheep and cattle. Mounted men were many, and there was something of a town, with a lake and a church.

Today it is a land of sandhills, stony deserts and salty clay-pans, with boiling soda-water bores fuming in the landscape and flowing like miniature rivers into polygonum swamps. A land where stone tools and nardoo mills, fallen yards and the bones of thousands of cattle, and ruined homesteads and the whitened skeletons of humans lie half-buried in the sand. There are only half a dozen white settlers and a score of civilized aborigines left in it.

Madigan was a geologist. With Sir Douglas Mawson he had found traces of potash to the north-west of this sand-ribbed desert area. Some say he was disappointed in not finding valuable salt deposits on the dry bed of Lake Eyre North and consequently did not wish others to share a like disappointment. It may be so—or he may even have missed that for which he was looking and those valuable deposits may still lie on the lake bed. Or they may lie either on the other existing or older lake beds or somewhere else in this desert area. In any case, one day some hard-headed people will spurn the Professor's suggestion and consider it worth while to investigate further, and it is not unlikely that their efforts may meet with better success.

In one sense, however, Madigan was definitely right. For settlement purposes the whole of this sand-ribbed desert area is not worth a further thought. Until man can bring water from the clouds it is as dead as the dodo.

THE ATACAMA DESERT

LAKE SAGARIS

Poet and journalist Lake Sagaris was born in Montreal in 1956 and holds a BFA in Creative Writing from the University of British Columbia. In 1981, she moved to Chile to become a correspondent for the Miami *Herald* and *Newsweek*, among others. In 1996, she published *After the First Death: A Journey Through Chile, Time, Mind,* which documented the aftermath of Augusto Pinochet's 1973 coup through interviews, stories, and personal experience, recreating Chilean society during a time of violence and terror. Ariel Dorfman called it "a lucid, heart-wrenching journey into the troubled heart of my country." In *Bone and Dream: Into the World's Driest Desert* (2000), from which this passage is taken, she uses similar techniques to bring the Atacama Desert vividly to life in space and time. She imagines the past through the eyes of an Incan woman, Huillac Nusta, and the present by means of her own internal and external journeys, both set against the backdrop of the Atacama's haunting history.

IN DECEMBER 1995, armed with a couple of assignments, I once again entered the Atacama. Flying toward Calama, a flat, gritty town 1,566 kilometers north of Santiago, I was struck by how the land looks river-carved: enormous ravines rumbling down from the Andes toward the ocean, cliffs and clefts slashed by flash-floods thousands of years old, the surface rippling like sand in shallow water.

As our plane banked and glided earthward I studied the roads scarring the surface below me. Later, as Patricio, my companion, and I climbed into our rented car and shot toward a furred and empty heart of light, astonishment shivered along my nerves. We roared across a landscape of horizontal lines of violet and pink, pearly grey and steely blue, shifting, stretching, thinning under a relentless cobalt sky. We screeched to a halt by a roadside shrine, an animita, erected where some previous traveller had died. A tamarugal tree, the desert's weeping willow, trembled in the breeze, two feet tall. The attached sign pleaded, like those hanging round the necks of beggars in downtown Santiago, not for loose change, but for water.

As we wound through the last crystal peaks and down into the valley towards San Pedro de Atacama, the mountains of salt looked like works of art, charged with dramatic meaning. Lost voices keened along the hollows of my bones.

The landscape's very stillness seemed to shiver. This desert was breaking every rule of the imagination. The rocks proclaimed, *Your expectations make the landscape lie.* I had expected sand, but this was a land of stone and salt. I took the tufts of silver-plated grass for sheep huddled together. The tawny curves of lions' backs were golden moss; a prickly porcupine, some shrub; a jagged flock of birds, mere stones.

How many thousands of years, how many generations have measured these mountains with their feet, leaving their secrets buried under sand or marked by a lone figure standing out against the distance, transformed, as I approach, into a cairn?

The Atacama rises gently out of the Pacific Ocean, the world's largest body of water, but it is the driest desert on our planet. It stretches 970 kilometers north to south, starting from Arica at the Chile-Peru border and ending in Copiapo, about a third of the way down the long ladder that is Chile. There's nothing virgin or untouched about the Atacama. Rather, everyone and everything that has perished on its rocky plain or among its mountains of salt has left a mark.

For thousands of years, the bodies of those who ventured here shrivelled into the desert's surface of rock and bone, but their voices blended with the air. The desert is so silent that if you stand still, those voices come back to you, telling their stories: the Incas, expanding their empire southward through the mauve solitudes of rocks; the Aymara, the Chinchorros, the Atacamenians and the Diaguitas, building the oases which have made life possible; the conquistadors, dying in droves as they stumbled blindly over the scars left by others; the British businessmen, goading Chile into the War of 1879, by which Chile, and its English "patrons," seized control of the north's vast mineral wealth.

Before the Europeans reached this continent, the Atacama was sparsely populated, but heavily travelled by caravans linking the fishing and hunting peoples of the Pacific coast to the empires and isolated village oases of the high Andes nestling along what are today the border areas of Peru, Bolivia, Argentina and Chile. The main ethnic groups included the Diaguitas, known for their pottery of round bellies and precise geometrical designs in red, white and black; the fishing peoples known as the Changos, who lived not on the arid coast but in their canoes of inflated seal bladders, floating on the rolling surface of the sea, the Atacamenians, of the oases, and the Aymara, the former lords of the high Andes.

When, with the arrival of the Spanish, the map of the Incas' Andean empire shattered into individual settlements that were in turn gathered together again to form Spain's colonized kingdoms of Peru and Bolivia, the Atacama too was divided up. Peru grabbed the northernmost reaches, Chile the southernmost and Bolivia held on to a stretch that reached to the Pacific Ocean.

In the nineteenth century, the War of the Pacific (1879–1883) pitted Chile against Bolivia and Peru. The upshot was a Chilean victory, thanks in part to support from the British and a heritage of bitter distrust and contempt that underlies Chile's relations with Peru and Bolivia to this day. However, the war did bring the Atacama, with all its mineral wealth, into the sphere of Chileans eager to build if not an empire, at least a country, stretching from Arica at the Peruvian border, and the northern edge of the Atacama, all the way down to Punta Arenas and Tierra del

Fuego in the south. Once the war was over, the British nitrate mines fuelled prosperous towns—mere ghosts today—and a union movement that changed Chilean history.

Since the late eighties, American and now Canadian mining companies have been tearing out the desert's very entrails in their search for the high-grade copper, silver and gold that make the figures on their balance sheets shine. To do so, they often find themselves battling the surviving native people for the desert's lifeblood, water.

These are the bare facts, but they don't explain the way this seemingly empty tract of land has filled itself over the years with the sighs and shouts of past adventurers, how their whispering still moves the sun-shot air.

For five years, the Atacama desert has haunted me, a ghostly presence composed of majestic silence and brutal conflict, the shadows of men and women struggling to wrest a green shoot from its rocky surface or stumbling through palaces of ice to the golden mansions they hoped to build, their hearing assaulted by the strangled screams of massacres, the distant chime of hammer on stone, alarm bells, the warning buzz before the *tronadura*, the massive daily explosion that blasts free new ore to be trucked to the surface of its open-pit mines.

But there are also the shouts and laughter of giggling children as they slap and spray each other, crowding around the tap in the central square of San Pedro de Atacama. Another illusion shatters in the bright sunlight. Oases, at least here in the Atacama, are not found but built. Over thousand of years the channels were dug and lined with stones, then painstakingly cleaned and feasted over every year, to keep the water racing into the fertile ground. They mine these waters, loaded with salt and arsenic, like rock until they find enough to green the rushes and feed the hungry flocks of llama, donkeys, sheep. The water's poisonous, but still life survives.

The descendants of those who built the oasis still live there quietly, among the green fields sliced into neat rectangles by rows of poplars and high adobe walls.

SAN PEDRO DE ATACAMA's Central Square has become a key to the mental map that pins me to the earth. At one edge stands the Padre le Paige Museum, squat and white, its generator humming incongruously day and night, as if it were the motor that keeps the world spinning on its axis. The museum's contents offer a rather ironic tribute to human history as told by the surrounding earth. It makes everything look so easy, so accessible, even this desert seeded with thousands of mummies, preparing its bizarre crop. Some are the result of sophisticated effort, but most are natural, prepared by mourners, then dried and preserved by the land itself.

There were times on later visits when I would experience the museum as a relentless, godless kind of crypt, with its polished glass cases, the neatly printed labels, the locked doors behind which lurk headless bodies and lonely skulls, chipped rocks and weapons, the raw chaos of human detritus that gets shaped into its tidy presentations.

But that first time, I found marvels inside, sounds and sights that clung to my senses long after I returned to Santiago's pressured roar: golden objects that lie dented, scarred and crumpled as if someone had crushed them in his fist, tossed them away in rage. Among the earrings and beads, the golden headbands and ornaments, nine tiny vertebrae, a thousand years old, spelled out the brief life of a child.

In the central hall, a round chamber from which emanate the galleries that contain the museum's displays, lurked the shadows of lives trapped behind glass. In one large case, a woman's figure hunched over the ragged bundle of her newborn child. So lifelike was her pose that I could imagine the child growing up, running and shouting to friends, the mother grinding pestle against rock as she transformed nuts into flour, ears sharpened to her child's footfall or cry.

Such are the illusions of the museum curator's craft: this image of them, which rekindled movement in my mind's eye, was only the dried essence of a moment captured by the desert, in which death froze mother and child, ushering them forever out of life, at the moment of birth. Her dark braids, which made her feel so alive to me, had been neatly combed fifteen hundred years before, when someone wrapped her in a fine wool shawl and sang or said a last farewell.

That presence, those lives behind our lives, that sense of life surviving, penetrating death, the echoes of voices like radio waves filling the air, the sense, always that sense that this was a pregnant emptiness, shivering toward labour, bent on telling *something,* if someone would just tune in. It would call me back, over and over in the years to come, invisible threads tangled around my mind, tugging, gently, unforgiving. What or who was I searching for? Why?

She could be a woman, I thought, travelling from the heights of the altiplano to the lowlands of the coast, travelling from north to south, from triumph through failure to hope and death, and something after. From certainty to doubt. From presence to memory. From physical reality to myth. How would I know her, find her, and what could we possibly say to each other? The whole shape of her mind, her life, would be crafted by spirits and gods I might find interesting, but would not feel. At best a pagan atheist, in the Atacama I would be travelling through a landscape of faiths, every landmark a site for ritual prayers, offerings of spirits to spirits, candles lit to attract or deflect beings I could grasp like Joseph Campbell's myths, but could not experience as living forces.

I am a city creature, although I love the land. I love my tree-lined street, the bitter fight to hold a place for people against the neo-conservative logic that has tried to drive us from our homes. For almost as long as I've been obsessed by the Atacama, I've been fighting a highway project that would cut through our neighbourhood and our lives, severing the north bank of the Mapocho River—the historical heart of Santiago—from the rest of the city, forcing artists and writers, market vendors, professionals, retired workers out of our habitat, turning us into refugees in our own city. I'm addicted to

Internet and virtual worlds, the computer's synthetic mind and speed, the high-pitched tone of the fax machine at all hours of the night. Who would this woman be and why should I try to find her?

But in the end, there's not much point in arguing with an obsession. We don't choose them. They're born in us and drive us until we die. Like an addict eager for reform, I've tried to kick the writing habit many times. But here I am, terrified and fierce, setting out on another book, another journey, trying to create what I must find, because for some reason I can only sense, I can't live without it.

During that first visit to the anonymous woman's glass cage in the museum, there was a coda that I did not see: the parchment-like skin covered only her forehead and one cheek; on the other side of her face, white bones gleamed ruthlessly.

People here believe that the soul does not go to another land, Alonso Barros, a young lawyer working with the Atacamenian communities told me. *When one of these bodies is disturbed from their trip back to the Pachimama [earth], then the spirit emerges and starts to haunt those who have disturbed it.*

When I played back my tape from that first journey, what I noticed most were the sounds of water I had recorded, how it punctuated the wind, the voices, the tape's quiet hiss, shifted the meaning of everything I'd heard. The sound of a splash spilled out the memory of a fat, brown-skinned boy wearing a green T-shirt as he dove into the rock pool in the Atacamenian village of Peine. Past him, past the frame of giant ferns and primal shrubs around the pool, the horizon was an endless line of smoky rock and dust.

Then came the hissing geysers of Tatio, boiling up out of the earth, bringing the damp heat that swirled around me as I tried to wrap my shivers in those warm shrouds of steam, tried to absorb the heat, at 5:00 AM, 4,500 meters above sea level. On the way back down to San Pedro de Atacama, more bubbling, splashes and laughter even, to mark my discovery of Puritama, an Eden-like oasis complete with hot spring, dammed to provide shallow pools for chilly bathers.

Water is the source of life, said Barros. *Indigenous people have known that for a long time. It's part of their culture and their cosmovision. They worship water.*

But today, even as I sit down to write this, another well's gone dry in the heart of the Atacama salt fields. The water is vanishing—sucked up by the dry, hot skies, pumped out by lithium miners, gulped down by copper mines or piped away by water utilities trying to quench the bottomless thirst of coastal cities, their endless suburbs garnished with swimming pools.

We forget that deserts are results, not only of the massive geological changes the earth's crust has undergone, but also of the processes humankind can thoughtlessly unleash. Deforestation. Blasting. Building. Global warming. Every year, the desert's frontier creeps 500 meters farther south into Chile's fertile central valley.

Crucial moments of our history, as homo sapiens and peoples of the Americas, remain mummified, encrusted among its rocks and salt. Much of our future must lie there too, if we only knew how to read it. The desert lies wordlessly at our feet, speaks only through the peculiar objects it preserves, waiting for someone to pick them up, turn them over, listen with their fingertips.

SILENCE WAS its first gift to me, after fifteen years in noisy Santiago, where buses operate at 70 decibels and discotheques boom all night. After that silence, which cleansed the ears, I heard—water tinkling in a rusty culvert, children teasing each other, my footsteps crunching through the salty crust, memories of trudging to school in Canada among the frozen leaves.

And the desert has gone on, teaching me to experience anew, colour, space, texture: the guanacos—graceful Atacamenian camels—prancing together against a backdrop of brown velvet, or the green tongues of a plant, clinging to sand, fragile and stubborn as starlight.

Most of the landscapes I had known until then *like a mirror, turn you inward / And you become a forest in a furtive lake* as the poet, Gwendolyn MacEwen, wrote. But the desert turns you outward, stretches you beyond your skin.

On the last day of that first visit, we hurtled toward the Salar de Atacama, which is a shallow, briny lake shrinking amidst an enormous salt field. The rims of coastal mountains to our west deepened to blue, while in the east the peaks of Argentina smouldered, flared orange, dimmed to mauve. Further south loomed mountains of dust and steel. We stopped the car and stood alone on the vast plain of salt and brine, surrounded by a land composed of lines and shades of grey. The sharp scent of iodine rasped our nostrils. The faint cries of long-legged birds pecking at microscopic lives underlined not our solitude, but the solitary majesty of this place, graced by brilliant cerulean blues, the sharp pinks and greens of chemicals aflame, the gentle wash of yellow light soaking the skies, the hills, our eyes. When I gazed upward, the pink arrows with black-tipped wings that flung themselves across the sky were Andean flamingos.

Life and death live back to back, are halves of one whole. In the city, both crowd so close we cease to see them. Death seems unnatural. It usually takes us by surprise. Here, life stunned, delighted. And begged. In that salty heart of the world's driest desert, the flamingos lay their single annual egg in water, safe from rodents, birds of prey. But if the water evaporates, so does their fledgling future, and their kind.

Death is a shadow that always follows the body, an old English proverb says. In that bare and open plain, where the sun falls bright and even on every nook and rock, the line between earth and flesh has grown transparent. There is much to learn. Time and the land may look endless, but life is absolute and brief.

ANTOFAGASTA

ARIEL DORFMAN

Born in Buenos Aires and raised in New York, Ariel Dorfman moved to Chile with his family in 1954, when he was twelve. It was there that he "decided to reinvent myself as a Spanish speaker and Latin American patriot." He was exiled from Chile in 1973, when Pinochet's military coup ended the regime of Salvador Allende (Dorfman had been cultural and media adviser to Allende's chief of staff), but since the restoration of democracy in 1990, he once again makes his home in Santiago. Novelist, playwright, poet, and journalist, he is the author of numerous works, including the play *Death and the Maiden,* and a memoir, *Heading South, Looking North* (1998). In 2002, he and his wife Angélica traveled throughout Chile's El Norte Grande, a vast, barren desert where, he says, a person can live a lifetime without feeling a single drop of rain. This piece is from *Desert Memories: Journeys Through the Chilean North* (2004), his account of that momentous and memorable journey.

WE CLIMB INTO the car and head north.

"Next stop, Antofagasta," Angélica says, glad that we will not have to descend in darkness the cliffs that lead down to that port city by the sea.

I do not tell her that there is one more place I need to visit before Antofagasta, before the day is done. An antidote to the desert that I desperately need.

Not that I am put off by this drive. These last two days have been anything but monotonous. There are long hours, it is true, where nothing seems to change. But then suddenly there is a *cuesta,* a series of hills, like Portezuelo Blanco, and such a dizzying array of browns and grays and terra-cottas (Angélica's favorite color), all the hues that blend into each other and into something approaching whiteness farther on, and then a shining *arenal,* dunes of almost carrotlike pale red and then another granular slice of distance that wants to be the color of milk but can't quite manage it. And then there was a meseta made of darker clay, fingers and tongues of sand descending from it. And later a plain of such never-ending blue that it seems like the sea, seas of clay, seas of stone, seas of brownish blue, one of the few places in Chile so wide that you cannot see the Andes. Drunk with shades and pigments and tincture, so that I understand why so many come to the desert to get high on drugs and let themselves be gorged up through their eyes.

And then you are so very thankful when you see something as ordinary as a tiny tree, maybe it is a *tamarugo*—the species that used to cover parts of this desert and was used up to fuel the furnaces in the early days of the *salitreras;* and there is what seems to be a cactus, and farther on, that has to be a mirage in the desert, something like a city shimmering cloudlike on the horizon, no, no, it's—and then it disappears and your eyes focus on the road and what you're seeing can't be true either, but there is a man walking by himself on the other side of the road in the middle of nowhere, carrying a portable fridge on his side, the sort vendors have in stadiums at sports events and on the streets of the busiest intersections of cities, this man carting his ice cream around where nobody is there to buy and nobody to even stop and ask him what he's doing and I feel like buying something from him but we go on, we are consumed by the fever of the forward thrust of travel that often grips you when you are on limitless highways.

And *un arbolito,* Angélica exclaims excitedly—where the slightest surge of water appears and a tree next to it, that's where someone has built a house, the smallest of oases giving us some verdant hope. And close by, like a dog trailing a man, garbage, the refuse that follows our humanity around even in the desert. And side roads from time to time, inevitably lizarding off to a mine, abandoned or semi-functioning or about to be revived, the only reason why anybody would want to build a pathway in the middle of these shoals of dust.

And signs of the dead in the desert. *Animitas*—what you can find on every road in every corner of Chile but far more noticeable here because they stand out against the stark and barren background. Just about every six miles or so, a pile of stones, a cross, a sort of little chalklike sanctuary, in some cases even a miniature temple, to record where someone died violently and where it is presumed that the soul (the little soul, the animita) is still nearby, willing to intercede for the living with the gods or the Virgin or whoever commands the great beyond and can do favors for us. The small deaths and small dead that never made it into the cemeteries that begin to dot the horizon as we penetrate into the *salares* where nitrate towns sprang up. And then what seem to be mirrors lying flat for miles next to the highway, maybe satellite receivers and transmitters or devices to capture solar energy, so strangely, almost grotesquely, ultramodern in a desert where, if you deviate ten yards off the road, you'll find everything untouched and intact, exactly the way it was a million years ago.

Ways in which we try to mark the land as ours.

Messages in the desert. People who have come before us have stopped, picked up stones, reddish in color, and even redder contrasted with the wasted sand dunes behind them and used them to write their names by the side of the road—messages of love, short memories of hope and despair, dates, hearts. I feel a bizarre tenderness welling from inside me when we pass these words written on the skin of the desert, a melting away of the anger that graffiti in natural surroundings usually awakens in me, a comradeship with those people who touched the desert and left something, anything, embossed on its features, writing on the desert as if it were a page.

I was here, they are saying, *read me, I passed through . . .* Isn't that what I myself am here to do? Though I dream about penetrating its secrets, am I not just skimming the surface of this land in order to leave some sort of mark on it? Isn't this desert full of pictographs and petroglyphs and gigantic hieroglyphs left behind by its first inhabitants, the forerunners of the men and women at Monte Verde, didn't they also try to send a message we are still trying to decipher writing in their way on the desert with the elements provided, stones as words and stones for ideas, by that same desert?

And that is why I prepare to stop now, as we approach the interchange where we need to turn off the Panamericana and take the highway west that descends toward the sea and Antofagasta, seventy kilometers away, even if it is already darkening, even if we are late and our novelist friend is awaiting our call.

Up ahead, to one side of the route, is a gigantic granite hand thrusting up from a slight mound in the desert. Yes, I did say a granite hand and I did say gigantic—towering twenty or so meters high—a smooth rock statue, this *Mano,* erected here in 1992 by the Chilean sculptor Mario Irrarrázaval as a way of commemorating the presence of humans on this land, both the Europeans who had arrived in 1492 and those who had made the journey so many millennia before Columbus.

Our answer to the desert, that hand.

What makes us human. That we cannot accept the void, the nothingness. That we all want to leave something behind, a huella, a trace, but not by accident in the mud, not just a chance slip of a foot on the way to somewhere else, but deliberately, at times even brutally claiming what we find as ours.

There has to be a reason why writing was born on the edge

of the desert. Weren't the inhabitants of the great original civilizations that emerged in the river valleys only too aware of the dangerous wastes surrounding them? Wasn't writing invented as a way of seizing a piece of land—writing, in its beginnings, laying down the foundation of law but also establishing property rights, saying this piece of land is mine and not yours, and certainly not nature's, nature that writes its ownership of this Earth in ways different from men? Wasn't it fear of the emptiness that moved them? Fear of what the hollow rocks were telling us in those sands outside Caldera?

Trying to establish some form of permanence, that is what we do, this species.

All of us, living in ghost towns though we do not know it.

With the illusion that what we leave behind will not be swept away by the wind, that something will remain against the corrosion of time.

Hand by hand, hand in hand.

Gloriously making believe we will outlast the desert.

THE OLD GRINGO COMES
TO MEXICO TO DIE

CARLOS FUENTES

Born in Panama City in 1928, Mexican novelist Carlos Fuentes has written more than twenty books that have earned him the National Prize in Literature (Mexico's top literary honor), France's Legion of Honor, Italy's Grinzane Cavour Award, Spain's Prince of Asturias Award, and Brazil's Order of the Southern Cross. He was also Mexico's ambassador to France from 1975 to 1977. His novels include *The Death of Artemio Cruz* (1962), *The Years with Laura Diaz* (1999), and *The Old Gringo* (1985), from which the following account of the old gringo's passage into the Chihuahuan Desert is taken. The novel is Fuentes's interpretation of the disappearance of American journalist Ambrose Bierce; it deals with the clash of two cultures as well as with the idea of the desert as the unknown. "What you don't know is what you imagine," he has said.

. . .

STEEL-BLUE EYES BENEATH speckled, almost blond, eyebrows. They were not the best defense against the raging sun and the raw wind that the following day bore him into the heart of the desert, occasionally nibbling on a dry sandwich, setting a shapeless wide-brimmed black Stetson lower on his thatch of silvery hair. He felt like a gigantic albino monster in a world the sun had reserved for its favored, a people protected by darkness. The wind died down but the sun continued to burn. By afternoon, his skin would be peeling. He was deep in the Mexican desert, sister to the Sahara and the Gobi, continuation of the Arizona and Yuma deserts, mirror of the belt of sterile splendors girdling the globe as if to remind it that cold sands, burning skies, and barren beauty wait patiently and alertly to again overcome the earth from its very womb: the desert.

"The old gringo came to Mexico to die."

And nevertheless, plodding steadily forward on the white mare, he felt that his wish to die was a mockery. He surveyed the desert around him. Agave rose wiry and sharp as a sword's point. On every branch of the candlewood tree, thorns protected the untouchable beauty of a savagely red flower. The desert willow concentrated in a single pale, purplish flower all the sweetness of its nauseating perfume. The choya grew capricious and tall, shielding its yellow blossoms. The gringo may have come in search of Villa and the Revolution, but the desert was already the image of war: Spanish bayonet, war-like Apache plumes, and the aggressive, hook-like thorns of the palo verde. The desert's advance guard were its ranks of tumbleweed, botanical brothers to the packs of nocturnal wolves.

Buzzards circled above; the old man raised his head, then alertly looked toward the ground. In the desert, scorpions and snakes strike only at strangers. A traveler is always a stranger.

Dazed, he looked up, then down; he heard the mournful song of dark doves, swift as arrows, was confused by the flight of peregrine falcons. High overhead, birds trailed a sound like dry, rustling grass.

He closed his eyes but did not spur his horse.

Then the desert told him that death is nothing more than the exhaustion of the laws of nature: life is the rule of the game, not its exception, and even the seemingly dead desert hid a minute world of life that originated, prolonged, imitated the laws of human existence. He could not free himself—even if he wanted to—from the vital imperative of the barrenness to which he had come of his own free will, without anyone's having commanded: Old gringo, get you to the desert.

Sand mounts the mesquite. The horizon shimmers and rises before the eyes. Implacable shadows of clouds clothe the earth in dotted veils. Earth smells fill the air. A rainbow spills into a mirror of itself. Thickets of snakeweed blaze in clustered yellow blooms. Everything is blasted by an alkaline wind.

The old gringo coughs, covers his face with a black scarf. His breathing ebbs, as long ago the waters had drawn back from the earth to create the desert. He thirsts for air as salt cedars on parched stream banks treasure moisture.

He has to stop, choked by asthma, dismount painfully, gasping for breath, and devoutly sink his face into the mare's flank. In spite of everything, he says: "I am in control of my destiny."

Translation by Margaret Sayers Peden and Carlos Fuentes

THE DESERT
SMELLS LIKE RAIN:
AN OVERTURE

GARY PAUL NABHAN

Gary Paul Nabhan is a naturalist, ethnologist, and plant ecologist who has worked with Native American farmers in the Southwest to record and preserve their desert-adaptive traditions, especially in the area of food cultivation. Among his many books are *Coming Home to Eat: The Pleasures and Politics of Local Foods* (2001), *Why Some Like It Hot: Food, Genes and Cultural Diversity* (2004), and *Gathering the Desert* (1985), for which he won the John Burroughs Prize for Nature Writing. He is a McArthur Fellow, the director of Northern Arizona University's Center for Sustainable Environments, and a board member of Seed Savers Exchange. In his first book, *The Desert Smells Like Rain: A Naturalist in Papago Indian Country* (1982), the source of this excerpt, he takes the reader on a series of journeys through the traditional homelands of the Papago Indians of Arizona and Sonora, Mexico, sharing their foods, their sacred places, and their intimate knowledge of desert ecology.

LAST SATURDAY before dusk, the summer's 114-degree heat broke to 79 within an hour. A fury of wind whipped up, pelting houses with dust, debris, and gravel. Then a scatter of rain came, as a froth of purplish clouds charged across the skies. As the last of the sun's light dissipated, we could see Baboquivari Peak silhouetted on a red horizon, lightning dancing around its head.

The rains came that night—they changed the world.

Crusty dry since April, the desert floor softened under the rain's dance. Near the rain-pocked surface, hundreds of thousands of wild sprouts of bloodroot amaranth are popping off their seedcoats and diving toward light. Barren places will soon be shrouded in a veil of green.

Desert arroyos are running again, muddy water swirling after a head of suds, dung, and detritus. Where sheetfloods pool, buried animals awake, or new broods hatch. At dawn, dark egg-shaped clouds of flying ants hover over ground, excited in the early morning light.

In newly filled waterholes, spadefoot toads suddenly congregate. The males bellow. They seek out mates, then latch onto them with their special nuptial pads. The females spew out egg masses into the hot murky water. For two nights, the toad ponds are wild with chanting while the Western spadefoot's burnt-peanut-like smell looms thick in the air.

A yellow mud turtle crawls out of the drenched bottom of an old adobe borrow pit where he has been buried through the hot dry spell. He plods a hundred yards over to a floodwater reservoir and dives in. He has no memory of how many days it's been since his last swim, but the pull of the water—*that* is somehow familiar.

THIS IS the time when the Papago Indians of the Sonoran Desert celebrate the coming of the rainy season moons, the *Jujkiabig Mamsad,* and the beginning of a new year.

Fields lying fallow since the harvest of the winter crop are now ready for another planting. If sown within a month after summer solstice, they can produce a crop quick enough for harvest by the Feast of San Francisco, October 4.

When I went by the Madrugada home in Little Tucson on Monday, the family was eagerly talking about planting the flash-flood field again. At the end of June, Julian wasn't even sure if he would plant this year—no rain yet, too hot to prepare the field, and hardly any water left in their *charco* catchment basin.

Now, a fortnight later, the pond is nearly filled up to the brim. Runoff has fed into it though four small washes. Sheet-floods have swept across the field surface. Julian imagines big yellow squash blossoms in his field, just another month or so away. It makes his mouth water.

ONCE I ASKED a Papago youngster what the desert smelled like to him. He answered with little hesitation:

"The desert smells like rain."

His reply is a contradiction in the minds of most people. How could the desert smell like rain, when deserts are, by definition, places which lack substantial rainfall?

The boy's response was a sort of Papago shorthand. Hearing Papago can be like tasting a delicious fruit, while sensing that the taste comes from a tree with roots too deep to fathom.

The question had triggered a scent—creosote bushes after a storm—their aromatic oils released by the rains. His nose remembered being out in the desert, overtaken: *the desert smells like rain.*

MOST OUTSIDERS are struck by the apparent absence of rain in deserts, feeling that such places lack something vital. The Papago, on the other hand, are intrigued by the unpredictability rather than the paucity of rainfall—theirs is a dynamic, lively world, responsive to stormy forces that may come at any time.

A Sonoran Desert village may receive five inches of rain one year and fifteen the next. A single storm may dump an inch and a half in the matter of an hour on one field and entirely skip another a few miles away. Dry spells lasting four months may be broken by a single torrential cloudburst, then resume again for several more months. Unseasonal storms, and droughts during the customary rainy seasons, are frequent enough to reduce patterns to chaos.

The Papago have become so finely tuned to this unpredictability that it shapes the way they speak of rain. It has also ingrained itself deeply in the structure of their language.

Linguist William Pilcher has observed that the Papago discuss events in terms of their probability of occurrence, avoiding any assumption that an event will happen for sure:

. . . it is my impression that the Papago abhor the idea of making definite statements. I am still in doubt as to how close a
rain storm must be before one may properly say *t' o tju:* (It is
going to rain on us), rather than *tki ' o tju: ks* (something like:
It looks like it may be going to rain on us).

Since few Papago are willing to confirm that something will
happen until it does, an element of surprise becomes part of
almost everything. Nothing is ever really cut and dried. When
rains do come, they're a gift, a windfall, a lucky break.

Elderly Papago have explained to me that rain is more than
just water. There are different ways that water comes to living
things, and what it brings with it affects how things grow.

Remedio Cruz was once explaining to me why he plants the
old White Sonora variety of wheat when he does. He had waited
for some early January rains to gently moisten his field before he
planted. "That Pap'go wheat—it's good to plant just in January
or early February. It grows good on just the *rain*water from the
sky. It would not do good with water from the *ground,* so that's
why we plant it when those soft winter rains come to take care
of it."

In the late 1950s, a Sonoran Desert ecologist tried to sim-
ulate the gentle winter rains in an attempt to make the desert
bloom. Lloyd Tevis used untreated groundwater from a well,
sprayed up through a sprinkler, to encourage wildflower germination on an apparently lifeless patch of desert. While Tevis
did trigger germination of one kind of desert wildflower with

a little less than two inches of fake rain, none germinated with less than an inch. In general, production of other wildflowers required more than three or four inches of fake rain.

Tevis was then surprised to see what happened when less than an inch of real rain fell on his experimental site in January. He noticed in the previously sparse vegetation "a tremendous emergence of seedlings. Real rain demonstrated an extraordinary superiority over the artificial variety to bring about a high rate of germination." With one particular kind of desert wildflower, seedlings were fifty-six times more numerous after nearly an inch of real rain than they were after the more intense artificial watering.

The stimulating power of rain in the desert is simply more than moisture. Be it the nutrients released in a rainstorm, or the physical force of the water, there are other releasing mechanisms associated with rainwater. But even if someone worked up a better simulation of rain using *fortified* groundwater, would it be very useful in making the desert bloom?

Doubtful. Remedio himself wonders about the value of groundwater pumping for farming, for water is something he *sings* rather than pumps into his field. Every summer, Remedio and a few elderly companions sing to bring the waters from the earth and sky to meet each other. Remedio senses that only with this meeting will his summer beans, corn, and squash grow. A field relying solely on groundwater would not have what it takes. He has heard that well water has some kind of "medicine" (chemical) in it that is no good for crops. In addition, he believes that groundwater pumping as much as twenty miles away adversely affects the availability of moisture to his field.

I joined in a study with other scientists to compare the nutritive value of tepary beans grown in Papago flashflood fields with those grown in modern Anglo-American-style groundwater-irrigated fields nearby. The protein content of the teparies grown in the traditional flashflood environments tended to be higher than that of the same tepary bean varieties grown with water pumped from the ground. Production appeared to be more efficient in the Papago fields—more food energy was gained with less energy in labor and fuel spent. No wonder—it is a way of agriculture that has fine-tuned itself to local conditions over generations.

There they are, Julian and Remedio—growing food in a desert too harsh for most kinds of agriculture—using cues that few of us would ever notice. Their sense of how the desert works comes from decades of day-to-day observations. These perceptions have been filtered through a cultural tradition that has been refined, honed, and handed down over centuries of living in arid places.

If others wish to adapt to the Sonoran Desert's peculiarities, this ancient knowledge can serve as a guide. Yet the best guide will tell you: there are certain things you must learn on your own. The desert is unpredictable, enigmatic. One minute you will be smelling dust. The next, the desert can smell just like rain.

BAJA CALIFORNIA

ELLEN MELOY

Ellen Meloy (1946–2004) lived in Montana, Utah, and among the "chive-green" lawns of California for much of her life, and was most at home in the Mojave and Sonoran deserts. She was the author of numerous books on desert matters, including *The Anthropology of Turquoise: Meditations on Landscape, Art and Spirit* (2003), for which she was nominated for a Pulitzer Prize and won the Banff Mountain Book Festival Award. In *Eating Stone: Imagination and the Loss of the Wild* (2006), from which this account of her visit to the Baja Peninsula is taken, she records her obsession with desert bighorn sheep, a species that, like the desert that holds it, is very near extinction. "Homo sapiens," she writes, "have left themselves few places and scant ways to witness other species in their own world, an estrangement that leaves us hungry and lonely." Three months after completing *Eating Stone*, she died in her sleep at her home in Bluff, Utah.

. . .

UNDER A SAPPHIRE sky, the inland desert fills a broad valley in all directions, hemmed only by mountains that rise so abruptly from the flats, you would knock your forehead on them if you walked toward them blindfolded. Jagged white veins zig-zag through their brown faces, giving them the look of giant chunks of raw agate. A shallow arroyo furrows the valley's low-est point. Haloed by the low sun, *cardón* and cholla cover the land in a swathe of glowing bristles.

This gulf of open desert between ribs of mountains soothes the bone and muscle needed to cross it. There is a balance between sky and terra firma; they are complementary mirrors of infinity. Here, forms and shapes reveal themselves through patient inquiry and the luxury of enough carried water to let you trace them. Beyond the horizon lies the azure sea if we need it.

The truck lurches over a scant track. Near the arroyo, Mark puts it into four-wheel drive to cross the rough and pitted gravel of erosion. Often, Joe and I get out and walk in order to avoid suffering concussions on the truck cab's roof, and to feel the air. In another season, we would be baked to leather, babbling about milk shakes or waterfalls or swimming pools before we dived headfirst into the ground for one last mouthful of sand.

We have seen no one. The valley is uninhabited. The last structure sighted was a roofless cement block sprouting anten-nae of bare rebar, waiting in forlorn desolation for the construc-tion workers to come back from their ten-year lunch break.

The truck crawls up the valley. I am noticing high, bold faces of rock that are bighorn country. I am not noticing that the valley ends ahead of us, squeezed into a narrow slot in the mountains. The airy dreaminess of open desert pinches into a tight black crack. From where we are, the crack feels like dis-tance, but here, in this valley, distance breeds mirage.

Sixty miles back, before we left the main road, we encountered a man who told us about this arroyo and how it is a watering place for bighorns. He also spoke of a graveyard in the sierra in the opposite direction.

The *borrego cimarrón,* he said, go to that place to die. He pointed to mountains overlaid in blue on blue until the farthest layer was only slightly less pale than air. It is not a watering place, he insisted, but a bone place; scattered skeletons, curled horns, teeth and femurs and spines, rib cages with the wind in them. I cannot tell you more about this graveyard and I am not sure why.

Just short of the black crack, the arroyo is as wide as a riverbed. A narrow ribbon of water meanders down its course but soon disappears into the sand. A snow-white crust of dried salt lines the stream's edges. The water runs clear over settled minerals the color of rust.

We are heading into the crack, into a gorge of jagged night-dark rock. The stream flows there, too, and sheep tracks come to the water from nowhere. Each time we trace the tracks away from the water, they vanish. I do not want to enter the gorge, but Mark and Joe do, and they pull me along the slipstream of their curiosity.

A mile inside the gorge, we park the truck and make camp. Any farther and the road would be nearly impassable, and none of us is fond of pushing vehicles through dry streambeds or streams, even if they are streams of salt and sulfur. Others have driven this way, but their tracks are faint and weathered. There are signs of old mines, of the earth's skin torn off. This reckless exposure may be what gives the gorge its ominous air.

Before dinner, we hike up-canyon to look for signs of big-horn or the bighorns themselves. At one point the black gorge opens to softer walls of gold and red, and something tight around my chest loosens. Around a bend, we find scattered palm trees, fan palms with stocky trunks, a thatch of wild grasses in their shade, and rustling fronds that hint of paradise.

There is good sheep habitat here: water, food, bedding places, and escape terrain above the canyon and in a far-off spine of mountains turning to indigo in the evening light. Wherever you think the vertical rock is impossible, that is where you may find desert bighorns.

In his natural history of Baja California, written in the mid-1700s, Jesuit missionary Miguel del Barco related the curious acrobatics of the peninsular bighorn. As native hunters pursue a sheep, he wrote, "the sheep approaches the edge of a precipice and jumps off, taking care to land squarely on his head so that his thick horns can absorb the impact of the fall. Once down, he gets up and runs away." From the heights, the hunters look down "without venturing themselves to attempt a similar trick." The horns are so well made, Barco remarked, the sheep's entire head can take the blow of the fall without injury.

I have seen Blue Door Band sheep make extraordinary leaps. When they slip, they never flatten themselves, legs splayed, and claw for footholds as they slide. Instead, when they lose a foot-hold, they land on one below it, or the one below that. I have never seen one land on its head. They prefer not to show me this trick.

We leave the fan palms and turn back to camp. Mark and I hike the arroyo. Joe takes the talus above us, looking for signs of sheep until the walls become too steep and he must either descend to join us or be rimrocked.

How much work for all that meat, how difficult it must be to hunt them, I think. We cannot even *find* them. The most skilled hunters could herd an animal toward their *compadres,* who waited with bows and arrows, only to watch their prey fling itself into thin air, flying into the abyss, horns-first.

BACK IN camp, the wind begins. Soon it blows with the fury of something trapped, bottlenecked inside this narrow gorge, desperate to get out. The wind tries to blow our dinners off our plates. The wind pushes my discomfort into an ill-tempered gloom.

I do not like this place, I tell Mark, although the reasons elude me. The *banditos* are back in town, drinking tequila. The ax murderer cracked his differential en route. Monsters prefer swamps so that they can drip. In the list of terrors in creepy places, that leaves only the dreaded inner storm known as Self.

The rock is glassy and dark; the walls struggle with the light. Between the canyon walls, the sandy arroyo is hardly two hundred feet wide, and this is the space, so narrow and grim, like an earthquake fault in a primordial schist brain, that we inhabit.

The wild of this desert is a wild held intact by its own raw hostility, a reminder of nature's capacity to awe as well as kill you. Sunsets and bloodred ocotillo flowers and turquoise bays do no harm. I am neither hungry nor thirsty, nor am I punctured with thorns. I have the luxury of attention to insistent beauty. I live in a universe of sensation. But I could not survive here.

The wind cannot find its way out. It tears at our clothes and hair with nothing to temper its howl and grit. A stocky elephant tree barely shelters our bedroll. The night thickens into sepulchral dark. When the full moon rises, it weighs too much. I try to make the canyon into thoughtless space.

After our long sojourn on the sea and wide-open *bajadas*, it seems strange that we have come here. It is a choice that can be undone, I propose, but Mark and Joe want more reasons to change camp than the pathetic assertion that the rock is the wrong color.

Before sleep, we sit together on the sand with boulders for backrests. Joe tells us a bedtime story.

One of the things they did as kids growing up in southern Colorado, he says, was hunt for arrowheads. They searched land as flat as a pancake, chewed and cut and fenced to something entirely different from its original short-grass prairie but still yielding, once in a while, artifacts from its grassland past.

"My brothers and I were pretty young when we went arrowhead hunting," Joe begins, "maybe ranging in age from five to eight years old. Sometimes our sister went, but it usually was just the boys. Our father woke us up early in the morning. He had us dress in jeans and long-sleeved shirts and cowboy hats."

"The felt hats with the white braid looped on the edge of the brim? The cord chin straps with the wooden bead toggle?" I ask.

"Yes, those kids' cowboy hats," Joe replies. His voice is slow and deliberate, careful with this memory.

"We put on our cowboy hats and our dad drove us out to the prairie to look for arrowheads. When we got out of the car, he made us cinch up our chin straps and tie bandannas around our faces, folded into a V over the nose and knotted in the back, like stagecoach bandits. We had to help my littlest brother tie his. Each of us had a pair of goggles. The prairie dust was horrible, so we had to be covered up. Dad made us hold hands so we wouldn't be separated.

"So, in our cowboy hats, kerchiefs, and little goggles, we three boys walked across the prairie, holding hands, following our father, who always walked ahead of us, searching the dirt for worked stone."

It is the Mexican night, not a Colorado prairie, that wraps itself around us, yet the imagination can so easily make this leap. Stories lead the mind to calmer waters.

Natives of the Sonoran Desert who remember hunting bighorn recall that before the hunt they sat quietly in the night, conversing softly, telling stories about fat animals but, out of caution, never mentioning wild sheep.

When they were growing up in Montana, Mark and his siblings had those felt cowboy hats, I think as we slip into our sleeping bags beneath the moon. My brothers and I had those cowboy hats. Otherwise, we would have threatened to hold our breath or choke the family puppy until our parents gave in and bought them for us.

I CANNOT REMEMBER coffee, or putting on my sandals, or hiking down a chasm lined with purple shadows, leaving Mark and Joe to follow later. I only remember passing through the rocky portals and climbing the banks of the arroyo to the valley and the *bajadas,* to the sun.

My company is a scattered thatch of boojum trees and two coyotes. The low morning sun backlights trees and animals. Their auras—one of green leaves, the other of tawny fur—stand out in feline alertness. The coyotes are as lean as sticks. The ragged mountains float hazy blue on the horizons, holding sheep in their heights, occasionally spilling them into the dry washes, where the food grows. I am telling myself my own stories.

Older and beyond the cowboy hat phase, one of my brothers and I went through what I would call our "monk phase." Our family lived in Rome, Italy, at the time. Grant and I often explored the city's lesser-known churches, abbeys, and monasteries. Among our favorites was the eighteenth-century quarters of Jesuit priests, open to the public as a museum.

Off a long corridor of cool stone, each priest had a room nearly as slender as a closet, with whitewashed stucco walls, a narrow bed with a frayed blue cotton coverlet, a bloody crucifix, and a wooden desk by a window overlooking a lush courtyard garden.

This was the life we wanted, we decided; we'd be monks. Each of us would have an elegantly simple room with books and rolls of parchment and lots of paints and delicate sable brushes and a pen for inscribing our knowledge, which, as brainy Jesuits, would be vast and important. Silent brothers in robes and

Birkenstocks would bring us goblets of Chianti. The garden would soothe us. We would illuminate manuscripts.

It is this image that I bring to Father Piccolo in Baja California. His room overlooks orange and lemon trees. Its window frame is painted peacock blue. He is seated with his notebook. He writes exhaustive volumes on the local flora and fauna—cactus fifty feet tall, trees that loop, trees that look dead until rain teases them into full leaf. He writes of pearled shells. He writes of a horizon of azure sea and soil the color of poverty.

His manuscripts are illuminated with fish, fish swimming about the pages like chips of light, fish nosing the gold leaf of decorative script, swirling in schools through the loops of *Benedictus es*. He describes whales in the lagoons and the pronghorn antelope on the salt flats. He describes a cow-deer in the mountains. He refers to "precious pearls," never to anyone "wretched." He wears a deerskin cape in the morning chill.

My brother and I never became monks. Father Piccolo of Palermo likely did little of the above. Father Piccolo had an agenda. He had in mind the systematic evangelization of a wilderness people. He believed that lives so brief and full of misery needed the hope of heaven. Any fantasy that we might filter through three centuries obscures the blunt fact that the end result was genocide.

I would like to think that the right way to survive in this harsh desert is on the edge between wilderness and garden. The errant padres lived thus, yet they doomed the very culture that knew how to stay alive here, that knew how places like that black chasm could hold both food and fear.

Streamlining the complexities of history, you could say that, in livable areas, the padres left a legacy of irrigation and horticulture that sustained rural Baja California well into the twentieth century. One had to grow things. One had to be resourceful. The garden did not compromise the wild. This lifeway, too, is now ephemeral.

Today, we will leave the big arroyo and head north to the border, stopping to fish the bay with the yellowtail jack and sunlit islands—the sea, again—and to revisit the onyx spring, where we will find no sheep. We will bear home, triumphantly. . . a dog-eared postcard sold by a Mexican conservation group that helped introduce bighorns to Isla Tiburón across the Gulf.

The postcard shows a muscular bighorn ram on a pale granite outcrop, skylining in full profile. The Comcáac (Seri) of Isla Tiburón call the wild sheep *"mojet."* The Comcáac world is like a planet in a mirror of water, the tall cactus around them an ancient race of cape-wearing giants turned into *cardón*.

My field notes, my splintered mirror of this desert, are full of questions that will draw us back to Baja California to ask them again. My pages bulge with fish and palm trees and pomegranates in mission gardens, with ocotillos and boojums, the goat skeleton beneath the fallen *cardón* cactus. My notes are full of *mojet*.

Desert bighorns may bring you to places where they live, but they may not show themselves to you. This does not matter. What matters is this: Look.

THE GREAT
AMERICAN DESERT

EDWARD ABBEY

One of America's most passionate and prolific nature writers, Edward Abbey was born in Pennsylvania in 1927. In 1944, he moved to the Four Corners region, where the states of Arizona, Utah, Colorado, and New Mexico meet, and where, in his words, "the tangible and the mythical become the same." He worked as a winter ranger at Arches National Monument in the 1950s, and in 1968 published *Desert Solitaire,* a collection of essays and journal entries that has been compared to *Walden* for its impact on modern environmentalism. Indeed, his 1975 novel, *The Monkey Wrench Gang,* about a group of young "eco-warriors," inspired the Earth First! movement, although Abbey himself was no environmental activist. As Wendell Berry observed, Abbey believed that "our environmental problems are not, at root, political; they are cultural." His abiding love for the desert inspired thirteen more works of nonfiction, including *A Voice Crying in the Wilderness* (1989). This essay was first published in *The Journey Home* (1977). Abbey died in Arizona in 1989.

IN MY CASE it was love at first sight. This desert, all deserts, any desert. No matter where my head and feet may go, my heart and my entrails stay behind, here on the clean, true, comfortable rock, under the black sun of God's forsaken country. When I take on my next incarnation, my bones will remain bleaching nicely in a stone gulch under the rim of some faraway plateau, way out there in the back of beyond. An unrequited and excessive love, inhuman no doubt but painful anyhow, especially when I see my desert under attack. "The one death I cannot bear," said the Sonoran-Arizonan poet Richard Shelton. The kind of love that makes a man selfish, possessive, irritable. If you're thinking of a visit, my natural reaction is like a rattlesnake's—to warn you off. What I want to say goes something like this.

Survival Hint #1: Stay out of here. Don't go. Stay home and read a good book, this one for example. The Great American Desert is an awful place. People get hurt, get sick, get lost out there. Even if you survive, which is not certain, you will have a miserable time. The desert is for movies and God-intoxicated mystics, not for family recreation.

Let me enumerate the hazards. First the Walapai tiger, also known as the conenose kissing bug. *Triatoma protracta* is a true bug, black as sin, and it flies through the night quiet as an assassin. It does not attack directly like a mosquito or deerfly but alights at a discreet distance, undetected, and creeps upon you, its hairy little feet making not the slightest noise. The kissing bug is fond of warmth and like Dracula requires mammalian blood for sustenance. When it reaches you the bug crawls onto your skin so gently, so softly that unless your senses are hyperacute you feel nothing. Selecting a tender point, the bug slips its conical proboscis into your flesh, injecting a poisonous anesthetic. If you are asleep you will feel nothing. If you happen to be awake you may notice the faintest of pinpricks, hardly more than a brief ticklish sensation, which you will probably disregard. But the bug is already at work. Having numbed the nerves near the point of entry the bug proceeds (with a sigh of satisfaction) to withdraw blood. When its belly is filled, it pulls out, backs off, and waddles away, so drunk and gorged it cannot fly.

At about this time the victim awakes, scratching at a furious itch. If you recognize the symptoms at once, you can sometimes find the bug in your vicinity and destroy it. But revenge will be your only satisfaction. Your night is ruined. If you are of average sensitivity to a kissing bug's poison your entire body breaks out in hives, skin aflame from head to toe. Some people become seriously ill, in many cases requiring hospitalization. Others recover fully after five or six hours except for a hard and itchy swelling which may endure for a week.

After the kissing bug, you should beware of rattlesnakes; we have half a dozen species, all offensive and dangerous, plus centipedes, millipedes, tarantulas, black widows, brown recluses, Gila monsters, the deadly poisonous coral snakes, and giant hairy desert scorpions. Plus an immense variety and near-infinite number of ants, ticks, midges, gnats, bloodsucking flies, and blood-guzzling mosquitoes. (You might think the desert would be spared at least mosquitoes? Not so. Peer in any water hole by day: swarming with mosquito larvae. Venture out on

a summer's eve: The air vibrates with their mournful keen-
ing.) Finally, where the desert meets the sea, as on the coasts
of Sonora and Baja California, we have the usual assortment of
obnoxious marine life: sandflies, ghost crabs, stingrays, electric
jellyfish, spiny sea urchins, maneating sharks, and other creatures so distasteful one prefers not even to name them.

It has been said, and truly, that everything in the desert
either stings, stabs, stinks, or sticks. You will find the flora here
as venomous, hooked, barbed, thorny, prickly, needled, saw-
toothed, hairy, stickered, mean, bitter, sharp, wiry, and fierce
as the animals. Something about the desert inclines all living
things to harshness and acerbity. The soft evolve out. Except for
sleek and oily growths like the poison ivy—oh yes, indeed—
that flourish in sinister profusion on the dank walls above the
quicksand down in those corridors of gloom and labyrinthine
monotony that men call canyons.

We come now to the third major hazard, which is sunshine.
Too much of a good thing can be fatal. Sunstroke, heatstroke,
and dehydration are common misfortunes in the bright American Southwest. If you can avoid the insects, reptiles, and
arachnids, the cactus and the ivy, the smog of the southwestern
cities and the lung fungus of the desert valleys (carried by dust
in the air), you cannot escape the desert sun. Too much exposure to it eventually causes, quite literally, not merely sunburn
but skin cancer.

Much sun, little rain also means an arid climate. Compared
with the high humidity of more hospitable regions, the dry heat

of the desert seems at first not terribly uncomfortable—sometimes even pleasant. But that sensation of comfort is false, a deception, and therefore all the more dangerous, for it induces overexertion and an insufficient consumption of water, even when water is available. This leads to various internal complications, some immediate—sunstroke, for example—and some not apparent until much later. Mild but prolonged dehydration, continued over a span of months or years, leads to the crystallization of mineral solutions in the urinary tract, that is, to what urologists call urinary calculi or kidney stones. A disability common in all the world's arid regions. Kidney stones, in case you haven't met one, come in many shapes and sizes, from pellets smooth as BB shot to highly irregular calcifications resembling asteroids, Vietcong shrapnel, and crown-of-thorns starfish. Some of these objects may be "passed" naturally; others can be removed only by means of the Davis stone basket or by surgery. Me—I was lucky; I passed mine with only a groan, my forehead pressed against the wall of a pissoir in the rear of a Tuscan bar that I cannot recommend.

You may be getting the impression by now that the desert is not the most suitable of environments for human habitation. Correct. Of all the Earth's climatic zones, excepting only the Antarctic, the deserts are the least inhabited, the least "developed," for reasons that should now be clear.

You may wish to ask, Yes, okay, but among North American deserts which is the *worst*? A good question—and I am happy to attempt an answer.

Geographers generally divide the North American desert—
what was once termed "the Great American Desert"—into
four distinct regions or subdeserts. These are the Sonoran Desert, which comprises southern Arizona, Baja California, and
the state of Sonora in Mexico; the Chihuahuan Desert, which
includes west Texas, southern New Mexico, and the states of
Chihuahua and Coahuila in Mexico; the Mojave Desert, which
includes southeastern California and small portions of Nevada,
Utah, and Arizona; and the Great Basin Desert, which includes
most of Utah and Nevada, northern Arizona, northwestern
New Mexico, and much of Idaho and eastern Oregon.

Privately, I prefer my own categories. Up north in Utah
somewhere is the canyon country—places like Zeke's Hole,
Death Hollow, Pucker Pass, Buckskin Gulch, Nausea Crick,
Wolf Hole, Mollie's Nipple, Dirty Devil River, Horse Canyon,
Horseshoe Canyon, Lost Horse Canyon, Horsethief Canyon,
and Horseshit Canyon, to name only the more classic places.
Down in Arizona and Sonora there's the cactus country; if you
have nothing better to do, you might take a look at High Tanks,
Salome Creek, Tortilla Flat, Esperero ("Hoper") Canyon, Holy
Joe Peak, Depression Canyon, Painted Cave, Hell Hole Can-
yon, Hell's Half Acre, Iceberg Canyon, Tiburon (Shark) Island,
Pinacate Peak, Infernal Valley, Sykes Crater, Montezuma's Head,
Gu Oidak, Kuakatch, Pisinimo, and Baboquivari Mountain,
for example.

Then there's The Canyon. *The* Canyon. The Grand. That's
one world. And North Rim—that's another. And Death Valley,

still another, where I lived one winter near Furnace Creek and climbed the Funeral Mountains, tasted Badwater, looked into the Devil's Hole, hollered up Echo Canyon, searched for and never did find Seldom Seen Slim. Looked for *satori* near Vana, Nevada, and found a ghost town named Bonnie Claire. Never made it to Winnemucca. Drove through the Smoke Creek Desert and down through Big Pine and Lone Pine and home across the Panamints to Death Valley again—home sweet home that winter.

And which of these deserts is the worst? I find it hard to judge. They're all bad—not half bad but all bad. In the Sonoran Desert, Phoenix will get you if the sun, snakes, bugs, and arthropods don't. In the Mojave Desert it's Las Vegas, more sickening by far than the Glauber's salt in the Death Valley sinkholes. Go to Chihuahua and you're liable to get busted in El Paso and sandbagged in Ciudad Juárez—where all old whores go to die. Up north in the Great Basin Desert, on the Plateau Province, in the canyon country, your heart will break, seeing the strip mines open up and the power plants rise where only cowboys and Indians and J. Wesley Powell ever roamed before.

Nevertheless, all is not lost; much remains, and I welcome the prospect of an army of lug-soled hiker's boots on the desert trails. To save what wilderness is left in the American Southwest—and in the American Southwest only the wilderness is worth saving—we are going to need all the recruits we can get. All the hands, heads, bodies, time, money, effort we can find. Presumably—and the Sierra Club, the Wilderness Society, the Friends of the Earth, the Audubon Society, the Defenders of

Wildlife operate on this theory—those who learn to love what is spare, rough, wild, undeveloped, and unbroken will be willing to fight for it, will help resist the strip miners, highway builders, land developers, weapons testers, power producers, tree chainers, clear cutters, oil drillers, dam beavers, subdividers—the list goes on and on—before that zinc-hearted, termite-brained, squint-eyed, near-sighted, greedy crew succeeds in completely californicating what still survives of the Great American Desert.

So much for the Good Cause. Now what about desert hiking itself, you may ask. I'm glad you asked that question. I firmly believe that one should never—I repeat *never*—go out into that formidable wasteland of cactus, heat, serpents, rock, scrub, and thorn without careful planning, thorough and cautious preparation, and complete—never mind the expense!—*complete* equipment. My motto is: Be Prepared.

That is my belief and that is my motto. My practice, however, is a little different. I tend to go off in a more or less random direction myself, half-baked, half-assed, half-cocked, and half-ripped. Why? Well, because I have an indolent and melancholy nature and don't care to be bothered getting all those *things* together—all that bloody *gear*—maps, compass, binoculars, poncho, pup tent, shoes, first-aid kit, rope, flashlight, inspirational poetry, water, food—and because anyhow I approach nature with a certain surly ill-will, daring Her to make trouble. Later when I'm deep into Natural Bridges Natural Moneymint or Zion National Parkinglot or say General Shithead National Forest Land of Many Abuses why then, of course, when it's a bit late, then I may wish I had packed that something extra: matches perhaps, not to mention one useful item, or maybe a spoon to eat my gruel with.

If I hike with another person it's usually the same; most of my friends have indolent and melancholy natures too. A cursed lot, all of them. I think of my comrade John De Puy, for example, sloping along for mile after mile like a goddamned camel—indefatigable—with those J.C. Penny hightops on his feet and that plastic pack on his back he got with five books of Green Stamps and nothing inside it but a sketchbook, some home-made jerky and a few cans of green chiles. Or Douglas Peacock, ex-Green Beret, just the opposite. Built like a buffalo, he hefts a ninety-pound canvas pannier on his back at trailhead, loaded with guns, ammunition, bayonet, pitons and carabiners, cameras, field books, a 150-foot rope, geologist's sledge, rock samples, assay kit, field glasses, two gallons of water in steel canteens, jungle boots, a case of C-rations, rope hammock, pharmaceuticals in a pig-iron box, raincoat, overcoat, two-man mountain tent, Dutch oven, hibachi, shovel, ax, inflatable boat, and near the top of the load and distributed through side and back pockets, easily accessible, a case of beer. Not because he enjoys or needs all that weight—he may never get to the bottom of that cargo on a ten-day outing—but simply because Douglas uses his packbag for general storage both at home and on the trail and prefers not to have to rearrange everything from time to time merely for the purposes of a hike. Thus my friends De Puy and Peacock; you may wish to avoid such extremes.

A few tips on desert etiquette:

1. Carry a cooking stove, if you must cook. Do not burn desert wood, which is rare and beautiful and required ages for its creation (an ironwood tree lives for over 1,000 years and juniper almost as long).

2. If you must, out of need, build a fire, then for God's sake allow it to burn itself out before you leave—do not bury it, as Boy Scouts and Campfire Girls do, under a heap of mud or sand. Scatter the ashes; replace any rocks you may have used in constructing a fireplace; do all you can to obliterate the evidence that you camped here. (The Search & Rescue Team may be looking for you.)

3. Do not bury garbage—the wildlife will only dig it up again. Burn what will burn and pack out the rest. The same goes for toilet paper: Don't bury it, *burn it*.

4. Do not bathe in desert pools, natural tanks, *tinajas*, potholes. Drink what water you need, take what you need, and leave the rest for the next hiker and more important for the bees, birds, and animals—bighorn sheep, coyotes, lions, foxes, badgers, deer, wild pigs, wild horses—whose *lives* depend on that water.

5. Always remove and destroy survey stakes, flagging advertising signboards, mining claim markers, animal traps, poisoned bait, seismic exploration geophones, and other such artifacts of industrialism. The men who put those things there are up to no good and it is our duty to confound them. Keep America Beautiful. Grow a Beard. Take a Bath. Burn a Billboard.

Anyway—why go into the desert? Really, why do it? That sun, roaring at you all day long. The fetid, tepid, vapid little water holes slowly evaporating under a scum of grease, full of cannibal beetles, spotted toads, horsehair worms, liver flukes, and down at the bottom, inevitable, the pale cadaver of a ten-inch centipede. Those pink rattlesnakes down in The Canyon, those diamondback monsters thick as a truck driver's wrist that lurk in shady places along the trail, those unpleasant solpugids and unnecessary Jerusalem crickets that scurry on dirty claws across your face at night. Why? The rain that comes down like lead shot and wrecks the trail, those sudden rockfalls of obscure origin that crash like thunder ten feet behind you in the heart of a dead-still afternoon. The ubiquitous buzzard, so patient—but only so patient. The sullen and hostile Indians, all on welfare. The ragweed, the tumbleweed, the Jimson weed, the snakeweed. The scorpion in your shoe at dawn. The dreary wind that blows all spring, the psychedelic Joshua trees waving their arms at you on moonlight nights. Sand in the soup du jour. Halazone tablets in your canteen. The barren hills that always go up, which is bad, or down, which is worse. Those canyons like catacombs with quicksand lapping at your crotch. Hollow, mummified horses with forelegs casually crossed, dead for ten years, leaning against the corner of a barbed-wire fence. Pack-horses at night, iron-shod, clattering over the slickrock through your camp. The last tin of tuna, two flat tires, not enough water and a forty-mile trek to Tule Well. An osprey on a cardón cactus, snatching the head off a living fish—always the best part first. The hawk sailing by at 200 feet, a squirming snake in its talons. Salt in the drinking water. Salt, selenium, arsenic, radon and radium in the water, in the gravel, in your bones. Water so hard it bends light, drills holes in rock and chokes up your radiator. Why go there? Those places with the hardcase names: Starvation Creek, Poverty Knoll, Hungry Valley, Bitter Springs, Last Chance Canyon, Dungeon Canyon, Whipsaw Flat, Dead Horse Point, Scorpion Flat, Dead Man Draw, Stinking Spring, Camino del Diablo, Jornado del Muerto . . . Death Valley.

Well then, why indeed go walking into the desert, that grim ground, that bleak and lonesome land where, as Genghis Khan said of India, "the heat is bad and the water makes men sick"?

Why the desert, when you could be strolling along the golden beaches of California? Camping by a stream of pure Rocky Mountain spring water in colorful Colorado? Loafing through a laurel slick in the misty hills of North Carolina? Or getting your head mashed in the greasy alley behind the Elysium Bar and Grill in Hoboken, New Jersey? Why the desert, given a world of such splendor and variety?

A friend and I took a walk around the base of a mountain up beyond Coconino County, Arizona. This was a mountain we'd been planning to circumambulate for years. Finally we put on our walking shoes and did it. About halfway around this mountain, on the third or fourth day, we paused for a while— two days—by the side of a stream which the Indians call Nasja because of the amber color of the water. (Caused perhaps by juniper roots—the water seems safe enough to drink.) On our second day there I walked down the stream, alone, to look at the canyon beyond. I entered the canyon and followed it for half the afternoon, for three or four miles, maybe, until it became a gorge so deep, narrow and dark, full of water and the inevitable quagmires of quicksand, that I turned around and looked for a way out. A route other than the way I'd come, which was crooked and uncomfortable and buried—I wanted to see what was up on top of this world. I found a sort of chimney flue on the east wall, which looked plausible, and sweated and cursed my way up through that until I reached a point where I could walk upright, like a human being. Another 300 feet of scrambling brought me to the rim of that canyon. No one, I felt certain, had ever before departed Nasja Canyon by that route.

But someone had. Near the summit I found an arrow sign, three feet long, formed of stones and pointing off into the north toward those same old purple vistas, so grand, immense, and mysterious, of more canyons, more mesas and plateaus, more mountains, more cloud-dappled sunspangled leagues of desert sand and desert rock under the same old wide and aching sky.

The arrow pointed into the north. But what was it pointing *at?* I looked at the sign closely and saw that those dark, desert-varnished stones had been in place for a long, long time; they rested in compacted dust. They must have been there for a century at least. I followed the direction indicated and came promptly to the rim of another canyon and a drop-off straight down of a good 500 feet. Not that way, surely. Across this canyon was nothing of any unusual interest that I could see—only the familiar sun-blasted sandstone, a few scrubby clumps of black-brush and prickly pear, a few acres of nothing where only a lizard could graze, surrounded by a few square miles of more nothingness interesting chiefly to horned toads. I returned to the arrow and checked again, this time with field glasses, looking away for as far as my aided eyes could see toward the north, for ten, twenty, forty miles into the distance. I studied the scene with care, looking for an ancient Indian ruin, a significant cairn, perhaps an abandoned mine, a hidden treasure of some inconceivable wealth, the mother of all mother lodes...

But there was nothing out there. Nothing at all. Nothing but the desert. Nothing but the silent world.

That's why.

SHOSHONE LAND

MARY AUSTIN

Born Mary Hunter in Illinois in 1868, Mary Austin traveled to California with her mother and brother in 1891 and married Stafford Austin, who discouraged her from writing. She nonetheless published *The Land of Little Rain*—a collection of her experiences with the Shoshone and Paiute of the Southwest desert regions—in 1903. The book, which includes this passage, was an immediate bestseller, although Austin was ejected from the Methodist Church for consorting with Indians. She went on to write thirty books, including the play *The Arrow-Maker* (1911), the novels *The Ford* (1917) and *Cactus Thorn* (which was not published during her lifetime), and the autobiography *Earth Horizon* (1932), before her death in 1934. She was an international literary figure: her friends included Jack London, Sinclair Lewis, Joseph Conrad, and Robert Frost. Her territory was the Sierra Nevada, Death Valley, and the Mojave Desert, and her theme was the necessity for human culture to be derived from the physical environment.

IT IS TRUE I have been in Shoshone Land, but before that, long before, I had seen it through the eyes of Winnenap' in a rosy mist of reminiscence, and must always see it with a sense of intimacy in the light that never was. Sitting on the golden slope at the campoodie, looking across Bitter Lake to the purple tops of Mutarango, the medicine-man drew up its happy places one by one, like little blessed islands in a sea of talk. For he was born a Shoshone, was Winnenap'; and though his name, his wife, his children, and his tribal relations were of the Paiutes, his thoughts turned homesickly towards Shoshone Land. Once a Shoshone always a Shoshone. Winnenap' lived gingerly among the Paiutes and in his heart despised them. But he could speak a tolerable English when he would, and he always would if it were of Shoshone Land.

He had come into the keeping of the Paiutes as a hostage for the long peace which the authority of the whites made interminable, and, though there was now no order in the tribe, nor any power that could have lawfully restrained him, kept on in the old usage, to save his honor and the word of his vanished kin. He had seen his children's children in the borders of the Paiutes, but loved best his own miles of sand and rainbow-painted hills. Professedly he had not seen them since the beginning of his hostage; but every year about the end of the rains and before the strength of the sun had come upon us from the south, the medicine-man went apart on the mountains to gather herbs, and when he came again I knew by the new fortitude of his countenance and the new color of his reminiscences that he had been alone and unspied upon in Shoshone Land.

To reach that country from the campoodie, one goes south and south, within hearing of the lip-lip-lapping of the great tideless lake, and south by east over a high rolling district, miles and miles of sage and nothing else. So one comes to the country of the painted hills, old red cones of craters, wasteful beds of mineral earths, hot, acrid springs, and steam jets issuing from a leprous soil. After the hills the black rock, after the craters the spewed lava, ash strewn, of incredible thickness, and full of sharp, winding rifts. There are no picture writings carved deep in the face of the cliffs to mark the way for those who do not know it. On the very edge of the black rock the earth falls away in a wide sweeping hollow, which is Shoshone Land.

South the land rises in very blue hills, blue because thickly wooded with ceanothus and manzanita, the haunt of deer and the border of the Shoshones. Eastward the land goes very far by broken ranges, narrow valleys of pure desertness, and huge mesas uplifted to the sky-line, east and east, and no man knows the end of it.

It is the country of the bighorn, the wapiti, and the wolf, nesting place of buzzards, land of cloud-nourished trees and wild things that live without drink. Above all, it is the land of the creosote and the mesquite. The mesquite is God's best thought in all this desertness. It grows in the open, is thorny, stocky, close grown, and iron-rooted. Long winds move in the draughty valleys, blown sand fills and fills about the lower branches, piling pyramidal dunes, from the top of which the mesquite twigs flourish greenly. Fifteen or twenty feet under the drift, where it seems no rain could penetrate, the main trunk grows, attaining often a yard's thickness, resistant as oak. In Shoshone Land one digs for large timber; that is in the southerly, sandy exposures. Higher on the table-topped ranges low trees of juniper and piñon stand each apart, rounded and spreading heaps of greenness. Between them, but each to itself in smooth clear spaces, tufts of tall feathered grass.

This is the sense of the desert hills, that there is room enough and time enough. Trees grow to consummate domes; every plant has its perfect work. Noxious weeds such as come up thickly in crowded fields do not flourish in the free spaces. Live long enough with an Indian, and he or the wild things will show you a use for everything that grows in these borders.

The manner of the country makes the usage of life there, and the land will not be lived in except in its own fashion. The Shoshones live like their trees, with great spaces between and in pairs and in family groups they set up wattled huts by the infrequent springs. More wickiups than two make a very great number. Their shelters are lightly built, for they travel much and far, following where deer feed and seeds ripen, but they are not more lonely than other creatures that inhabit there.

The year's round is somewhat in this fashion. After the piñon harvest the clans foregather on a warm southward slope for the annual adjustment of tribal difficulties and the medicine dance, for marriage and mourning and vengeance, and the exchange of serviceable information; if, for example, the deer have shifted their feeding ground, if the wild sheep have come back to Waban, or certain springs run full or dry. Here the Shoshones winter flockwise, weaving baskets and hunting big game driven down from the country of the deep snow. And this brief intercourse is all the use they have of their kind, for now there are no wars, and many of their ancient crafts have fallen into disuse. The solitariness of the life breeds in the men, as in the plants, a certain well-roundedness and sufficiency to its own ends. Any Shoshone family has in itself the man-seed, power to multiply and replenish, potentialities for food and clothing and shelter, for healing and beautifying.

When the rain is over and gone they are stirred by the instinct of those that journeyed eastward from Eden, and go up each with his mate and young brood, like birds to old nesting places. The beginning of spring in Shoshone Land—oh the soft wonder of it!—is a mistiness as of incense smoke, a veil of greenness over the whitish stubby shrubs, a web of color on the silver sanded soil. No counting covers the multitude of rayed blossoms that break suddenly underfoot in the brief season of the winter rains, with silky furred or prickly viscid foliage, or no foliage at all. They are morning and evening bloomers chiefly, and strong seeders. Years of scant rains they lie shut and safe in the winnowed sands, so that some species appear to be extinct. Years of long storms they break so thickly into bloom that no horse treads without crushing them. These years the gullies of the hills are rank with fern and a great tangle of climbing vines.

Just as the mesa twilights have their vocal note in the love call of the burrowing owl, so the desert spring is voiced by the mourning doves. Welcome and sweet they sound in the smoky mornings before breeding time, and where they frequent in any great numbers water is confidently looked for. Still by the springs one finds the cunning brush shelters from which the Shoshone shot arrows at them when the doves came to drink.

Now as to these same Shoshones there are some who claim that they have no right to the name, which belongs to a more northerly tribe; but that is the word they will be called by, and there is no greater offense than to call an Indian out of his name. According to their traditions and all proper evidence, they were a great people occupying far north and east of their present bounds, driven thence by the Paiutes. Between the two tribes is the residuum of old hostilities.

Winnenap', whose memory ran to the time when the boundary of the Paiute country was a dead-line to Shoshones, told me once how himself and another lad, in an unforgotten spring, discovered a nesting place of buzzards a bit of a way beyond the borders. And they two burned to rob those nests. Oh, for no purpose at all except as boys rob nests immemorially, for the fun of it, to have and handle and show to other lads as an exceeding treasure, and afterwards discard. So, not quite meaning to, but breathless with daring, they crept up a gully, across a sage brush flat and through a waste of boulders, to the rugged pines where their sharp eyes had made out the buzzards settling.

The medicine-man told me, always with a quaking relish at this point, that while they, grown bold by success, were still in the tree, they sighted a Paiute hunting party crossing between them and their own land. That was mid-morning, and all day on into the dark the boys crept and crawled and slid, from boulder to bush, and bush to boulder, in cactus scrub and on naked sand, always in a sweat of fear, until the dust caked in the nostrils and the breath sobbed in the body, around and away many a mile until they came to their own land again. And all the time Winnenap' carried those buzzard's eggs in the slack of his single buckskin garment! Young Shoshones are like young quail, knowing without teaching about feeding and hiding, and learning what civilized children never learn, to be still and to keep on being still, at the first hint of danger or strangeness.

As for food, that appears to be chiefly a matter of being willing. Desert Indians all eat chuck-wallas, big black and white lizards that have delicate white flesh savored like chicken. Both the Shoshones and the coyotes are fond of the flesh of *Gopherus agassizii*, the turtle that by feeding on buds, going without drink, and burrowing in the sand through the winter, contrives to live a known period of twenty-five years. It seems that most seeds are foodful in the arid regions, most berries edible, and many shrubs good for firewood with the sap in them. The mesquite bean, whether the screw or straight pod, pounded to a meal, boiled to a kind of mush, and dried in cakes, sulphur-colored and needing an axe to cut it, is an excellent food for long journeys. Fermented in water with wild honey and the honeycomb, it makes a pleasant, mildly intoxicating drink.

Next to spring, the best time to visit Shoshone Land is when the deer-star hangs low and white like a torch over the morning hills. Go up past Winnedumah and down Saline and up again to the rim of Mesquite Valley. Take no tent, but if you will, have an Indian build you a wickiup, willows planted in a circle, drawn over to an arch, and bound cunningly with withes, all the leaves on, and chinks to count the stars through. But there was never any but Winnenap' who could tell and make it worth telling about Shoshone Land.

And Winnenap' will not any more. He died, as do most medicine-men of the Paiutes.

Where the lot falls when the campoodie chooses a medicine-man there it rests. It is an honor a man seldom seeks but must wear, an honor with a condition. When three patients die under his ministrations, the medicine-man must yield his life and his office. Wounds do not count; broken bones and bullet holes the Indian can understand, but measles, pneumonia, and smallpox are witchcraft. Winnenap' was medicine-man for fifteen years. Besides considerable skill in healing herbs, he used his prerogatives cunningly. It is permitted the medicine-man to decline the case when the patient has had treatment from any other, say the white doctor, whom many of the younger generation consult. Or, if before having seen the patient, he can definitely refer his disorder to some supernatural cause wholly out of the medicine-man's jurisdiction, say to the spite of an evil spirit going about in the form of a coyote, and states the case convincingly, he may avoid the penalty. But this must not be pushed too far. All else failing, he can hide. Winnenap' did this the time of the measles epidemic. Returning from his yearly herb gathering, he heard of it at Black Rock, and turning aside, he was not to be found, nor did he return to his own place until the disease had spent itself, and half the children of the campoodie were in their shallow graves with beads sprinkled over them.

It is possible the tale of Winnenap's patients had not been strictly kept. There had not been a medicine-man killed in the valley for twelve years, and for that the perpetrators had been severely punished by the whites. The winter of the Big Snow an epidemic of pneumonia carried off the Indians with scarcely a warning; from the lake northward to the lava flats they died in the sweat-houses, and under the hands of the medicine-men. Even the drugs of the white physician had no power.

After two weeks of this plague the Paiutes drew to council to consider the remissness of their medicine-men. They were sore with grief and afraid for themselves; as a result of the council, one in every campoodie was sentenced to the ancient penalty. But schooling and native shrewdness had raised up in the younger men an unfaith in old usages, so judgment halted between sentence and execution. At Three Pines the government teacher brought out influential whites to threaten and cajole the stubborn tribes. At Tunawai the conservatives sent into Nevada for that pacific old humbug, Johnson Sides, most notable of Paiute orators, to harangue his people. Citizens of the towns turned out with food and comforts, and so after a season the trouble passed.

But here at Maverick there was no school, no oratory, and no alleviation. One third of the campoodie died, and the rest killed the medicine-men. Winnenap' expected it, and for days walked and sat a little apart from his family that he might meet it as became a Shoshone, no doubt suffering the agony of dread deferred. When finally three men came and sat at his fire without greeting he knew his time. He turned a little from them, dropped his chin upon his knees, and looked out over Shosone Land, breathing evenly. The women went into the wickiup and covered their heads with their blankets.

So much has the Indian lost of savageness by merely desisting from killing, that the executioners braved themselves to their work by drinking and a show of quarrelsomeness. In the end a sharp hatchet-stroke discharged the duty of the campoodie. Afterward his women buried him, and a warm wind coming out of the south, the force of the disease was broken, and even they acquiesced in the wisdom of the tribe. That summer they told me all except the names of the Three.

Since it appears that we make our own heaven here, no doubt we shall have a hand in the heaven of hereafter; and I know what Winnenap's will be like: worth going to if one has leave to live in it according to his liking. It will be tawny gold underfoot, walled up with jacinth and jasper, ribbed with chalcedony, and yet no hymn-book heaven, but the free air and free spaces of Shoshone Land.

STEER GULCH

ANN ZWINGER

Writer and artist Ann Haymond Zwinger was born in Muncie, Indiana, in 1925, and graduated in art history from Indiana University in 1950. Shortly thereafter she moved to Colorado, where her love and knowledge of art combined with a natural affinity for the desert and literature. In 1970, she published her first book, *Beyond the Aspen Grove*, and since then has written and illustrated eighteen works of natural history, including *Run, River, Run* (1975), for which she won the John Burroughs Medal; *Wind in the Rock* (1978), from which the following account of her sojourns in the desert canyons of the Colorado River is taken; *The Near-Sighted Naturalist* (1998); and *Shaped by Wind and Water: Reflections of a Naturalist* (2000). She lives in Colorado Springs, Colorado.

. . .

THE SIGNS OF recent water continue encouraging. A little bullsnake slithers down the wash, so rattlesnakes, too, can still be out. Thick crusts of salt crunch underfoot. Puffy and white and spiny, the salt leached out of shales in the Halgaito

Formation to the north. Rocks are coated, ground encrusted with it; even the drainage lines on the sand are crystalline white. Often there is wet silt hidden beneath, which makes one very wary of walking on it.

The channel deepens imperceptibly and begins to narrow. The banks become high enough to obscure the countryside. Five mule deer bound off ahead in stiff-legged jumps. When I reach their hoofprints, the impress is slurred in the silt, deeply impressed and elongated with their hurry. One of them is a buck with a beautiful wide set of antlers, rising high and handsome from his forehead.

Mule deer were an important food source for the Anasazi, and were relatively plentiful in this area, being able to utilize a wide number of plant species. Although they are fleet of foot and spend most of the day, except early morning and evening, undercover, they also follow the same trails day after day through the small home range, rendering themselves vulnerable to the observant hunter who waited in ambush.

Puddles and pools become more frequent: graininess of sand gives way to shine of silt and glint of water. On exposed bedrock long continuous pools gleam, a foot or so wide and up to thirty feet long, opulent parabolas and sinuous ellipses, an interplay of convexity and concavity, of sandstone and water.

Two monstrous boulders, fifteen feet high, shaped like two vertebrae, are so set together that they relate to each other, curve and hollow, bellied and bowed, like a Henry Moore sculpture. Arches cut through each and a narrow alleyway winds

through the middle so that I can stand inside. One bears a
scapula-like thin ledge. So bonelike in contour are these rocks
that one immediately envisions the beast from which they came:
a huge ponderous creature, not ill-hearted, lumbering across
the desert, leaving a canyon for a footprint.

Large rocks ahead mark the confluence of the main channel of Steer Gulch with a side drainage. When we finally reach
them they flank large potholes, filled with water so slightly settled out that it looks like liquid sandpaper. When water charges
down this canyon during flash flood it carries with it a considerable amount of sand. Flowing down a bedrock channel, the
water slides across the flatter reaches with slowed current; then,
because of jointing or crossbedding in the rock that forms a step
or dropoff, it picks up speed and abrasive capacity, swirling its
sand load into every depression, enlarging and rounding it out
to a pothole basin. The size and the shape vary: some are circu-
lar bowls, others elongated basins, some scalloped ovals, com-
monly not deeper than a few feet.

We take the water bottles out of our packs, drink, then hold
the bottles upside down and listen to the water gurgle and glug
out. I have a momentary panic when I think that there may be
no more pothole water, but weigh the evidence of these pools
against carrying that much extra weight and trust in the logic of
knowing at least there is water here and available.

Strangely enough, even though the water in my cup looks
like bleached tomato soup, it isn't bad drinking. All the water
for the cattle that were run here came from potholes. The name

Steer Gulch refers to the cowboy practice of storing steers here. Two roundups were made yearly, the major one in June, when the cattle were drifted up to higher country for the summer, and a second one in October, when cattle were brought down. Because of the paucity of plant cover, cattle raising in this area depends upon the use of massive acreages and shifting cattle about according to the season. In the fall, calves were weaned and branded, and marketable stock was culled out to be sold. An old cowboy camp still remains under an overhang at the junction of a tributary canyon with Steer Gulch proper, with enough artifacts inside to indicate long habitation—even a mattress.

CAMP IS SET in the curve of the canyon, rock wall on the outer side, sand bar on the inner. A stunted cottonwood draped with debris documents the height of the last flash flood through here. Its big thick leaves rattle in the breeze. Rabbitbrush, so named because it is favored cover for these animals, flowers in huge tangles. A wide-ranging species, its bloom is familiar throughout the West. Because it is common on overgrazed lands and where other cover is sparse, its great masses often make a splendid show of color. A yellow dye is made by the Indians from the flowers, and the stems are occasionally used in wickerwork and as a kiva fuel—why I cannot imagine, for rabbitbrush gives off a viscous sooty smoke that I find quite unpleasant. Perhaps this is due to the rubber content of the plant; it has been estimated that, if recoverable, there are 300 million pounds of good-grade rubber blooming in the arid West.

Golden asters and a single rich deep-lavender tansy aster are flowering in warm protected crevices; even the tumbleweed seems to be in bloom, its papery bracts resembling thin parchment flowers with pink centers. Summer still seems to persist into October although the wind is more restless, as in fall. But between gusts there is a deep, warm honey stillness that holds the waning afternoon close and warm. Out here I feel keenly the pivoting of the seasons, all the plants that betoken fall, the sun warmth reminiscent of summer, the looping, buzzing fly not yet stilled, the snow not yet fallen. Each day, each place is a fulcrum of passage, a moment held for a few hours before tumbling forward with a cruel gust of wind and a crushing frost.

That night a full moon balloons over the canyon wall. I count: eighty seconds from the first chink of light on the rock horizon to the appearance of a full round globe, cold and white. Cold light and cold night, with a steely stillness. Not a breeze stirs to mix the air. No cloud cover holds in residual heat and reduces nocturnal radiation. The reality of autumn sinks in, as the cold air just flows in and lays itself down and mantles everything. A cricket sings for a moment, but it's more a pulsation than a singing, so slow and reluctant. And all night long the whole canyon gleams, as if dipped in silver.

IN THE MORNING a tentative dawn breeze doesn't even nudge the cottonwood leaves but sends a sharp chill down the canyon. The sky is a pale lavendar gray with no hint of the warmth to come. Getting out of the sleeping bag before the sun is out takes an act of courage. When it finally blasts over the sandstone wall I feel warmed and alive and energized and agree with Nels Nelson, the archaeologist who traveled down Grand Gulch in 1920: "Wonderful stillness of a sunny morning following a cold night—no bird or insect making a sound."

Around my ground cloth the sand is untracked; the night was too cold for lizards to go foraging. But a kangaroo rat was here—while packing up I discover its little corpse, front feet drawn up much as they are in life, tail with a minute shaving-brush tuft of fur at the end. I have no idea why it died. Having only seen them on the run at night, I take the opportunity to look at this little creature with care. Its back legs are long and well-muscled for jumping, and the long tail with its brave banner provides balance. By swinging its tail it can make rapid plunges in either direction, and up to ten-foot leaps.

Its ear openings are large, gathering in subtle sounds that presage danger. More than half of its skull is an air chamber, thought to catch and magnify sound vibrations in much the same way as an ear trumpet. The ears are protected from dirt by hooded tips. There is also a small lobe that closes over the ear opening when the kangaroo rat digs.

I poke around to see if I can discover an open den nearby, since they are usually noticeable if one knows where to look, often a mound of excavated earth topping a many-tunneled burrow beneath ground, containing nests and storerooms and feeding places. During the hot summer days the many entrances are closed to prevent loss of humidity; all food gathering is done at night. The doorways are usually quite large, as befits an owner who often escapes being someone else's dinner by getting home on a dead run.

Because a kangaroo rat is so vulnerable to the other hunters of the night—the horned owl's silent approach on velvet-barbed wings, the coyote's quick pounce and snap—it only gathers its seeds, not eating until safe in its nest. It carries the seeds in fur-lined cheek pouches (the kangaroo rat is like the pocket gopher in this respect) that open along the line of the lower jaw and hold about a teaspoonful each. It stuffs the pouches with quick movements, cramming in seeds, chaff, husks, and all, and empties them with a single paw push from the back.

Kangaroo rats are exquisitely fitted to living in dry areas because of a complicated chemical process that creates free water from the metabolic breakdown of food. Consequently they do not need to drink, securing all the moisture they need from their diet. Breeding is probably keyed to the amount of food available and occurs erratically. After breeding the male is expected to depart; if not he is more than likely killed by the female.

Three or four young are usually born in the spring, when food plants are at their most succulent, and so I would guess the tiny creature alongside my boot could be five or so months old. The newborn are helpless: hairless, eye and ear openings covered, no teeth, soft claws, but at two and a half months they are apparently full grown, although they retain their juvenile coats; by four months they are adult. Such rapid maturing is a necessity in a desert environment in which future survival often depends upon the quick gathering and storing of sufficient food that appears briefly after a good rain.

Kangaroo rats avoid water. To keep clean they take sand baths. A small gland on top of the shoulders secretes an oily substance that soon mats the hair; a good sand bath returns gloss and shine. They are fastidious creatures, and even in death the little fellow has a clean white vest and a neat tail brush.

WALKING UP a side channel, we find it necessary to traverse a steep wall in order to miss an eighty-foot dry waterfall around the corner. As I climb up through rock and rubble, half scrambling, half walking, a big horned owl flares out of some brush and scares the daylights out of me. In a quarter mile the waterfall is visible far below.

The whole canyon floor up here is a still life. When it is dry, it's a clean palette, but when damp, a sampling of desert life appears: spidery seed heads and single yellow blossoms from rabbitbrush; a tumbleweed sprig standing on one barb; deer hoofprints deep with scattered sand at the margins; coyote tracks in a wandering casual line; a minute blackbrush leaf; a gnarled cottonwood twig; a yellow cottonwood leaf, caught at the tip, browning at the veins.

Ahead a spotted ground squirrel scampers across the shiny pavement. It seems to fly, scarcely touching the ground. When I get there, the tiny footprints just tick the crest of the silt ripples. Slightly bigger than a chipmunk, the spotted ground squirrel is seldom seen except in motion. It feeds on the myriad desert seeds, and often lives in overgrazed areas invaded by tumble-weeds. (The only other ground squirrel in this area is a white-tail antelope squirrel, but it runs with its tail curled up over its back, showing the white underside.)

Dark holes at the base of some of the shrubs along the channel side catch my eye, regular shapes against the irregularity of the shadows, likely ground-squirrel diggings. They are nearly all on the shaded north side, burrowed into hummocks of sand that have blown up around the base of the shrubs, the cool side chosen for protection against the heat of summer. I try to peer inside or to listen, but there are no sounds of residence, and I lack the courage to poke a finger in. Were it an inhabited kangaroo-rat or pocket-mouse burrow, the door would most likely be plugged with dirt. If an abandoned burrow, it could house a snake, a scorpion, or poisonous spider, with none of which do I care to shake hands.

Animal life here is characterized by swiftness, like the fleet lizard or bounding kangaroo rat or scampering ground squirrel. Jumping or leaping gaits are common among small animals. Predator and prey alike have highly developed powers of hearing, perhaps because tracks are constantly covered with blown sand, smells mixed and lost by the wind and the constant shifting of the ground. Many desert animals are nocturnal, lizards and ground squirrels being two of the exceptions. And many burrow, as do the mice and many spiders and other insects. Most are closely adapted to the hues of the landscape—the lizard and the rattler patterned like the weathered, shadow-splotched sandstone, the ground squirrel speckled, even the coyote the buffy color of the country rock.

At times like this I feel my clumsy humanness, clomping along on feet that are not my own, unable to survive on the land for long, an interloper, an interrupter, a frightening shadow caster and ground shaker.

AS I WALK up this wing of the canyon, the walls come closer and closer, reaching up higher and higher without a break, and then the canyon ends against a box wall, blocked by a dry waterfall with no passage to the rim above. While someone looks for a route, I choose to sit here, facing a monolithic curved wall hollowed out with niches and depressions in which the water once spun, subtle convolutions that cradle soft-edged shadows.

The back wall flutters with reflections from the plunge pool that fills the last twenty twisty feet. The back of the pool rests in shadow, the front in sun, breathing without wind, bedecked with a few water striders that punctuate the warm cinnamon brown of the water. The reflection of the walls in the water is perfect, curve opening below to curve closing above, even reflections of the reflections, so that I cannot tell which is mirror, which is image, which is real, which is dream. But in all its beauty is a certain stubbornness, a place that resists passage, that forces you to go back in order to go on, a small inviolate ending.

Yet here after hiking eight miles with a heavy pack, in this stubborn stillness is one of the reasons for which I come to the canyons—these few minutes of quiet, of solitude, of absolute solace. No cricket chirrs, no water pounds, no stone falls. Time stands still and then expands. I feel my breathing become timed to that of the pool.

IT TURNS out that getting up from here means walking back an eighth of a mile or so, roping my pack up, climbing huge end-on boulders, stepping across a crevice with a thirty-foot drop below, and then traversing a sloping rock surface that would brook no slip.

We stop in the afternoon at a possible campsite, leave packs, and go exploring, coming across, in the middle of nowhere, half a dozen rusted-out cans and a cairn placed by the U.S. General Land Office Survey in 1927. A high butte a quarter mile away presents an incredible horizon-to-horizon view, low continuous horizons, so far away that they are beyond reaching, and if one walked a thousand years one would never get there.

A quarter mile away the streambed is lined with cottonwoods, and so perhaps has more water and is a better campsite than where the packs were left. But once there, the campsite is not propitious. The continual search for the perfect place to set up camp is a variation of "the grass is always greener" theme.

After some hot, dusty miles of walking hither, thither, and lots of yon, pothole bathing and privacy are worth selling one's soul for. The pothole that is my lot is not much bigger than a bathtub and in it I am submerged up to the chin. The depression is one of several in a rock chute, showing the lines of sandstone crossbedding in short repeated curves, moiré in stone. The water is at least sun-warmed on the surface. I upset the water striders, which flee up the sides with the sloshing; in deference to their delicate sensibilities I soap up and rinse off outside.

After dinner I walk up a nearby rock knoll. Wearing sneakers after boots makes my feet feel practically weightless. Last light washes the land. To the southwest Navajo Mountain glows, paler at the base, incandescent. No wonder the Navajos consider it a magic mountain. It has a symmetry, a serenity, that contrasts with the more fanciful landmarks like the Bears Ears or the markers of Monument Valley to the south. The realization of this tremendous emptiness closes in, of being miles from what is already nowhere, with a view that seems to reach farther than one can perceive. Perhaps the world *does* drop off beyond the rim.

Rock and more rock as far as I can see. And sand. And desolation. And mosquitoes. Fierce mosquitoes—I wish we'd had a good frost to put them under. But not even they can dim this time of peacefulness. In other canyons there are other concentrations: the fascination of ruins in Grand Gulch, the presence of more recent past in Johns and Slickhorn. But here there is nothing. Nothingness. And I find myself responding through every pore to this serenity, to the purity of this landscape.

THE RAVEN

BARRY LOPEZ

Essayist and short-story writer Barry Holstun Lopez was born in Port
Chester, New York, in 1945. He is perhaps best known for his 1986
book *Arctic Dreams*, but he is equally at home writing about deserts. His
trilogy—*Desert Notes* (1976), from which this excerpt is taken; *River
Notes* (1979); and *Field Notes* (1994)—explores the degrees to which landscape and culture intertwine, the many ways in which the one influences
the other: "What I'm trying to get at all the time," he writes, "is to examine the big questions," one of which is: "What is the relationship between
human culture and place?" He has contributed to many magazines, including *Harper's*, *Orion*, and *Outside*, and he has also written fiction, the most
recent being *Resistance* (2004). His book *Of Wolves and Men* (1978) won
the John Burroughs Medal and introduced the concept of pteraphobia, or
fear of animals, to the lexicon of human/wilderness encounters. Lopez cur-
rently lives in the Cascade Mountains of Oregon.

I AM GOING to have to start at the other end by telling you this: there are no crows in the desert. What appear to be crows are ravens. You must examine the crow, however, before you can understand the raven. To forget the crow completely, as some have tried to do, would be like trying to understand the one who stayed without talking to the one who left. It is important to make note of who has left the desert.

To begin with, the crow does nothing alone. He cannot abide silence and he is prone to stealing things, twigs and bits of straw, from the nests of his neighbors. It is a game with him. He enjoys tricks. If he cannot make up his mind the crow will take two or three wives, but this is not a game. The crow is very accommodating and he admires compulsiveness.

Crows will live in street trees in the residential areas of great cities. They will walk at night on the roofs of parked cars and peck at the grit; they will scrape the pinpoints of their talons across the steel and, with their necks outthrust, watch for frightened children listening in their beds.

Put all this to the raven: he will open his mouth as if to say something. Then he will look the other way and say nothing. Later, when you have forgotten, he will tell you he admires the crow.

The raven is larger than the crow and has a beard of black feathers at his throat. He is careful to kill only what he needs. Crows, on the other hand, will search out the great horned owl, kick and punch him awake, and then, for roosting too close to their nests, they will kill him. They will come out of the sky on a fat, hot afternoon and slam into the head of a dozing rabbit and go away laughing. They will tear out a whole row of planted corn and eat only a few kernels. They will defecate on scarecrows and go home and sleep with 200,000 of their friends in an atmosphere of congratulation. Again, it is only a game; this should not be taken to mean that they are evil.

There is however this: when too many crows come together on a roost there is a lot of shoving and noise and a white film begins to descend over the crows' eyes and they go blind. They fall from their perches and lie on the ground and starve to death. When confronted with this information, crows will look past you and warn you vacantly that it is easy to be misled.

The crow flies like a pigeon. The raven flies like a hawk. He is seen only at a great distance and then not very clearly. This is true of the crow too, but if you are very clever you can trap the crow. The only way to be sure what you have seen is a raven is to follow him until he dies of old age, and then examine the body.

Once there were many crows in the desert. I am told it was like this: you could sit back in the rocks and watch a pack of crows working over the carcass of a coyote. Some would eat, the others would try to squeeze out the vultures. The raven would never be seen. He would be at a distance, alone, perhaps eating a scorpion.

There was, at this time, a small alkaline water hole at the desert's edge. Its waters were bitter. No one but crows would drink there, although they drank sparingly, just one or two sips at a time. One day a raven warned someone about the dangers of drinking the bitter water and was overheard by a crow. When word of this passed among the crows they felt insulted. They jeered and raised insulting gestures to the ravens. They bullied each other into drinking the alkaline water until they had drunk the hole dry and gone blind.

The crows flew into canyon walls and dove straight into the ground at forty miles an hour and broke their necks. The worst of it was their cartwheeling across the desert floor, still wings outstretched, beaks agape, white eyes ballooning, surprising rattlesnakes hidden under sage bushes out of the noonday sun. The snakes awoke, struck and held. The wheeling birds strew them across the desert like sprung traps.

When all the crows were finally dead, the desert bacteria and fungi bored into them, burrowed through bone and muscle, through aqueous humor and feathers until they had reduced the stiff limbs of soft black to blue dust.

After that, there were no more crows in the desert. The few who watched from a distance took it as a sign and moved away.

Finally there is this: one morning four ravens sat at the edge of the desert waiting for the sun to rise. They had been there all night and the dew was like beads of quicksilver on their wings. Their eyes were closed and they were as still as the cracks in the desert floor.

The wind came off the snow-capped peaks to the north and ruffled their breath feathers. Their talons arched in the white earth and they smoothed their wings with sleek, dark bills. At first light their bodies swelled and their eyes flashed purple. When the dew dried on their wings they lifted off from the desert floor and flew away in four directions. Crows would never have had the patience for this.

If you want to know more about the raven: bury yourself in the desert so that you have a commanding view of the high basalt cliffs where he lives. Let only your eyes protrude. Do not blink—the movement will alert the raven to your continued presence. Wait until a generation of ravens has passed away. Of the new generation there will be at least one bird who will find you. He will see your eyes staring up out of the desert floor. The raven is cautious, but he is thorough. He will sense your peaceful intentions. Let him have the first word. Be careful: he will tell you he knows nothing.

If you do not have time for this, scour the weathered desert shacks for some sign of the raven's body. Look under old mattresses and beneath loose floorboards. Look behind the walls. Sooner or later you will find a severed foot. It will be his and it will be well preserved.

Take it out in the sunlight and examine it closely. Notice that there are three fingers that face forward, and a fourth, the longest and like a thumb, that faces to the rear. The instrument will be black but no longer shiny, the back of it sheathed in armor plate and the underside padded like a wolf's foot.

At the edge of each digit you will find a black, curved talon. You will see that the talons are not as sharp as you might have suspected. They are made to grasp and hold fast, not to puncture. They are more like the jaws of a trap than a fistful of ice picks. The subtle difference serves the raven well in the desert. He can weather a storm on a barren juniper limb; he can pick up and examine the crow's eye without breaking it.

GOING INTO THE DESERT

STEPHEN HARRIGAN

Stephen Harrigan was born in Oklahoma City in 1948, moved to Texas at the age of five, and began working as a staff writer for the *Texas Monthly* in 1975. He became interested in the way human beings and nature collide in their intentions, and his fiction often pits one against the other. The main character in his first novel, *Aransas* (1980), for example, is a dolphin trainer, and his 1984 novel, *Jacob's Well*, centers on an underwater cave that has claimed the lives of eight divers. His nonfiction mines similar terrain. For him, nature "always contained that hint of eeriness, the sense that some vital information... has been specifically withheld from me." This selection is from *A Natural State* (1988), a collection of essays published in *Texas Monthly* that explores regions of his adopted state that even his fellow Texans find wild and mysterious. Harrington now lives in Austin, where he is a fellow of the James A. Michener Center for Writers.

. . .

IT IS ONLY when the sun is low on the horizon that the desert takes on texture, becomes alluring in a conventional way. The shallow, sun-washed drainages begin to appear deep and inviting, places of refuge. The bleached arroyos that in the full light of day are nothing but impediments, that seem to criss-cross the desert floor without logic, suddenly are charged with significance and possibility. Subtle contours in the land become apparent, and in the variable light the solid components of the desert seem to shift and change shape like clouds. The wind is up. The temperature is down. The body, whose resources have been preoccupied all afternoon with preventing heatstroke, begins to make adjustments. As evening deepens, you can feel the blood enlivening your brain once again, and you feel that, instead of coming to the end of a tiring day, you are rising from a long and stupefying sleep.

A little nighthawk, a poorwill, flies low over the scrub, emitting plaintive bursts of song. There is a watery, musky smell— the diluted essence of skunk—that indicates a javelina is nearby, blundering about with its inferior eyesight. The subdued colors of the desert fade, except for a strawberry pitaya flower, which continues to burn like a flame until there is no light to support it. Mosquitoes, bred in the drying puddles of a nearby arroyo, circle ceaselessly around your head and bore into your eardrums with their whine. It is the last thing you want in this contemplative landscape, to be annoyed. Tonight the desert is as pretty as it is powerful—filled with minuscule, bothersome life as well as silent beasts who keep their thoughts to themselves as they stalk their prey on the ground or from the air. Vega is bright, and Venus rises with the Twins beneath the moon. Half of the moon is in shadow, and half is startlingly clear, glowing with eerie intensity, like the all-seeing eye of an owl. That is the real desert. In comparison with the moon, even the volcanic soil beneath your sleeping bag feels alive and impatient. A large beetle scuttles across your hand, mistaking it for a rock, for one more silent manifestation of the terrain.

THE DESERT rainy season, such as it is, occurs in the summer. The higher elevations can receive as much as twenty inches of rainfall a year, but in the lowlands the total is much less. The Chihuahuan Desert, by and large, lies beyond the reach of serious precipitation. Tucked away in the heart of a huge landmass, the desert is not on the itinerary of the big seasonal storms spawned in the Gulf and the Pacific. The rain systems that come its way are likely to be trapped by the mountain ranges that border the Chihuahuan for almost its whole extent. There the storms are broken up, the moisture-laden air retreating to windward and the rain shadow below receiving only a hot, evaporative wind.

But in the summer, thunderstorms often find their way to the desert. They're brief and volatile, drenching the unprepared soil and filling the dry washes with fast-moving sheets of floodwater. All sorts of things crawl out of the ground then, ready to feed and mate, to get on with a life that may have been held in suspension for months. I drove along a desert road recently after a rain. From my open window I could hear the bleating of what were probably spadefoot toads, and millipedes by the hundreds were crossing the road. Perhaps it was my imagination, but they all seemed to be crossing at the same angle; it was as if they were all single expressions of some larger impulse, some thought.

A desert tarantula was crossing the road as well. I stopped
the car and watched it. It was about six inches long and moved
slowly, probing with a pair of forelegs. Each step it took seemed
reasoned. I put my hand in its path, and it crawled up to my
wrist before thinking better of it and moving back to the asphalt.
Tarantulas are capable of inflicting a painful, mildly venomous bite, but if they are handled with consideration they're
extremely forbearing. Their abdomens are covered with a mat
of short, fine hairs—irritating to certain predators—which they
can shed when provoked.

Odds were that this tarantula, being on the prowl, was a
male. If he was sexually mature, he was at least ten years old.
His future was cloudy, however, given female tarantulas' pro-
pensity for eating their mates.

Tarantulas live on insects and other spiders, but they're
fully capable of pouncing on a creature as large as a mouse and
knocking it out with their venom. After that, they pump it full
of digestive juices and leisurely suck away its insides. The tarantula's mortal enemy is the tarantula hawk, a wasp that stings the
spider until it is comatose, then drags it off and uses it as a nest.
When the wasp's larvae hatch, they begin to consume the still-
living spider, bringing a protracted end to a life that may have
spanned 25 years.

As I drove I saw roadrunners, hunched forward in a kind of
Groucho Marx posture, speed across the highway in front of my
car, sometimes taking a short hop to the summit of a scrubby
mesquite. A large snake, bright pink, hurled itself at my tires. I
jerked the steering wheel back and forth and careened all over

the road trying to avoid it, feeling a little put out at the effort. I could have run over the snake and no jury in the world would have convicted me, but when I looked into the rearview mirror and saw it escaping into the brush unharmed I had to congratulate myself on my evasive driving skills. But the larger satisfaction was in not having caused a meaningless death, in not having insinuated my Buick Regal into the desert's balance of peril.

Up ahead a jackrabbit was perched tensely on the side of the road, waiting for whatever signal it needed to break and run. Its ears were enormous—they looked as if they were intended to gather data from outer space. The animal itself appeared gaunt and tested. When it finally took off, it crossed the road with astonishing speed, bounding forward on its immense hind legs. When it reached the other side it ran in zig-zags through the creosote and vanished under my gaze.

A jackrabbit is not a rabbit. It's a hare. Unlike rabbits, which are born naked in burrows, hares come into the world covered with fur, their eyes open, their minds already factoring the chances of escape over open ground. Jackrabbits survive by vigilance and speed. They live alone, sleeping in little scraped-out depressions, and the tiny indentations you often find along the edges of prickly pear pads are evidence that a jackrabbit has been feeding there.

Further on, another shape crossed the road. This was a canine, and I almost gasped at the thought it might be a wolf. Its haunches were scrawny, but it was larger than any coyote I'd ever seen, and it had a thick, reddish ruff at its neck. Its wildness was breathtaking. As it scrambled over a rise it reminded me of one of those wolves in Disney cartoons who appear on a mountaintop, ragged and lordly, in a flash of lightning.

But it could not have been a wolf. The last wolves in the Chihuahuan Desert disappeared, as far as anyone can tell, sometime in the early seventies, shot or crowded out or poisoned by sodium fluoroacetate. What I saw doubtless was a big coyote, but I didn't want to make myself believe it. I stopped the car and got out, savoring the image, and saw something even more arresting.

At first it seemed to be a rainbow, hovering low in a desert hollow three hundred yards away. It had rained a short time earlier, and the air was charged and complex, so a rainbow would not have been out of place. But that was not what this was. I could make out a few subtle gradations of the spectrum, but the phenomenon itself was a wonderful green light that had none of the phantom qualities of a rainbow. It was so well defined that I felt I could walk up to it and size it with a tape measure. I watched it, expecting something more. It was exactly the sort of supernatural light I had imagined as a boy in Catholic school, a backdrop from which the Virgin Mary might appear and say, as she always did in her apparitions, "Do not be afraid, my child."

The intricate atmospheric conditions that were causing this light could not be sustained for long, and in a moment it simply vanished, like water evaporating on a hot rock. I stared at the little arc of sky where it had been, greedy for something more, for some further revelation. I found it hard to take such a numinous display in passing. There was nothing mystical about it—it was neither hallucination nor vision—but when it was gone it lingered happily in my imagination, and I felt myself woven a little deeper into the fabric of the desert.

AFTER SEVERAL days of hiking around in the desert I began to wonder what it would be like to walk again in a landscape where every footstep did not have to be a considered proposition. One afternoon, on a rugged talus slope near the entrance to a narrow canyon, I came to the conclusion that it was not worth the effort to walk anymore. I felt like a contortionist as I tried to dodge the profusion of thorny plants surrounding me. Lechuguilla, prickly pear, pencil cactus, bloodroot, catclaw acacia, ocotillo—they were all savagely defending their precious stores of moisture, and I was sick of it. At that moment the desert was unsettling and grim, a place that preferred death over life. The bristly plants clung defiantly to the desert's surface, but if the desert itself had any one desire, it was to become a void.

To a degree, that is the course of things. The Chihuahuan Desert is threatened with "desertification." The more it is abused and degraded, the more it becomes a desert. To understand the tragic nature of this process, it's important to remember how intricate an environment a desert is. Deserts are second only to rain forests in their ability to support a wide variety of species. They have a range of climate and topography that creates more ecological niches than could exist in a temperate zone. But this natural diversity is fragile, and when it is stripped away, the desert loses all character and relief and becomes a monotonous, barren land.

· The threat comes from every direction. The grasslands are overgrazed, and in their place rise creosote and mesquite. Cowbirds that follow cattle onto the ranges lay their eggs in vireo nests, where the raucous cowbird chicks persuade the vireo mothers to feed them instead of their own young. A real estate development destroys bat' habitat, and because there are fewer bats to pollinate the century plant, its population declines. Running water is channeled or used up. Imported vegetation like salt cedar dries up a spring with its powerful hydraulics. The steady economic pressure on ranchers forces them to sell their land, which is subdivided for development. More wells are drilled, more water is depleted. More pesticides and contaminants are cycled into the food chain.

The Chihuahuan Desert Reseach Institute, which is headquartered in a portion of the science building at Sul Ross State University in Alpine, has been gamely trying to educate people through the years about the desert's variety and fragility. It's not an easy job, because the desert has no real constituency. People look out their car windows at the endless creosote plains and see emptiness. What they are looking at, however, is not the real desert in its vital and complicated glory. What they are looking at is what the desert has become.

THERE ON the talus slope, hemmed in by spines and needles, I was feeling less appreciative of the desert than I might have been. Maybe my cautious steps were a little exaggerated, but I was in one of those moods. The desert did not seem hostile, simply unconcerned about my welfare, and that was enough to make me feel vulnerable and alone.

So far, it had been a wet summer for this part of the desert, and the ocotillo plants I encountered—tall shrubs made up of dozens of thorny stems—were filled with leaves. A north wind began to whip the stems into motion, and I looked up to see the sky filled with separate thunderstorms, moving as ponderously as supertankers in a crowded harbor. All at once the atmosphere began to deepen, and the scraggly, denuded mountains in the distance turned steel-blue. I moved down to the flats, thinking to get back to the car, which was four miles away across the pathless scrub. I expected at any moment to be caught in a downpour, but soon it became apparent that it wasn't going to rain, that the great thunderheads were merely going to shuffle about on the horizon and disappear.

So I sat down to watch the spectacle of rain flirting with the desert. I took my Walkman out of my backpack, listened to Elvis Costello's *Imperial Bedroom* for a while, then switched to Schubert. The music brought the desert up a notch, or so I imagined. It imposed feeling and reason on a landscape that otherwise could be frighteningly neutral. Protected by Schubert, I perceived the desert's scale and stirrings in human terms. It seemed to want music as much as it wanted rain, and I felt that if I turned up the volume, life would explode from every burrow, from every pore in the calcified soil.

But after a point—when the ants near my feet appeared to be marching with renewed purpose and the wiry creosote stems were swaying in rhythm—the orchestration got to be too much. I took off the earphones and shrank right back into place— just one more creature with an overworked evaporative sys- tem, with no greater understanding of the desert than what my senses were able to tell me. Two Scott's orioles were singing to each other across the flats. When I stood up I startled a grass- hopper on a nearby mesquite, who took flight with a whirring sound that resembled the rattle of a snake. It reminded me to be cautious walking back. The thunderstorms were far away now, and the excitement had gone out of the atmosphere. There was only the sun, holding forth as usual. I took a long drink of warm water and felt just fine.

THE HOLINESS OF WATER

JOHN NICHOLS

Novelist and essayist John Nichols first moved to Taos, New Mexico, in 1969, and became one of the region's most ardent defenders. As editor of the *New Mexico Review*, he was a passionate advocate of an equitable water distribution system for Taos Valley farmers, a crusade that led to his celebrated novel (and later film) *The Milagro Beanfield War* (1974), the first of a trilogy that includes *The Magic Journey* (1978), and *The Nirvana Blues* (1981), which won the New Mexico Governor's Award. His nonfiction books include *If Mountains Die* (1979) and *In Praise of Mountain Lions* (1984), co-authored with Edward Abbey. The following essay, about the impact of water, is from *Dancing on the Stones* (2000), a wide-ranging collection that revisits the desert regions of the American southwest.

. . .

WHEN I WAS five and living in Montpelier, Vermont, at the end of World War II, I often visited a tiny pond in a small meadow overlooking town. The Tadpole Pond. It had a few cattails, maybe a lily pad or two, and lots of green algae. I was fascinated by the tadpoles, the dragonflies and darning needles, by the water skeeters and other aquatic life. The pond was only thirty feet across, a mere saucer of water. But it teemed with life. And I liked the scale, which was just my size as a child... and has remained so ever since. I don't know if that means I never grew up or if I am simply a spirit who sees most clearly when the view is limited and self-contained.

Today, at fifty-six, I am still connected to small puddles of water. I live in a dry country at high elevations far from Vermont. Mountains rise to thirteen thousand feet above my hometown and there is a fabled river gorge only a few miles west of the village plaza. Stretching for miles on either side of the river is a sagebrush mesa. Scattered across this parched land are a few stock ponds built ages ago by small ranchers in our valley. Three of those ponds, located within several miles of each other, have captivated me for years.

There are no trees beside the diminutive watering holes. The sun beats down without quarter, and when water accumulates it evaporates quickly. The tanks are splendid in their isolation, totally exposed to heat and wind and dust.

In a wet year I have seen them filled to overflowing, and the cañadas in which they lie boast turbulent muddy rivers. In a dry year the ponds are forlorn empty bowls, lackluster and desolate. It does not seem life could ever take hold in such a brutally mundane setting.

Yet I am drawn to these places of water in a sere landscape: the simplicity turns me on. The ponds are a metaphor that is clean. And I have visited them in all seasons, discovering count-less beautiful moods.

SOME DAYS on the mesa the wind blows until the air is laden with grit. Then it grows quiet and the sun beats down and even the sagebrush wilts. In the gut-wrenching heat, grasses wither and die and the air seems devoid of sufficient oxygen for breath-ing. It's hard to believe that animals, bugs, or birds could inhabit such alien country. There's no water in any of the stock ponds.

An impersonal majesty defines the arid realm, a kind of arc-tic desolation. But I can never travel through it without experi-encing an almost desperate yearning for rain. So my heart leaps up when I behold that first threatening puff of vapor in the sky.

All stock ponds are slave to this sky. They gain their being from springtime snowmelt or from sudden rain squalls when an entire small watershed delivers the goods. Thunderheads roll across the blue atmosphere like bison grazing a prairie; wind and lightning follow. When the clouds burst tons of moisture splat-ter to earth, but it takes a heap of rain to create even the tiniest pond. Imagine an atomic explosion whose energy is translated into a few square feet of water. The gods throw a virtual flood at the earth in order to create a single mosquito.

I have seen a pond fill to forty yards in length and half again as wide. On the mesa, that is a veritable lake, capable of breed-ing Loch Ness monsters. But for the most part my puddles remain small and are gone in several weeks. During that trun-cated season, however, all hell breaks loose.

ONE DAY many small white moths fluttered over a dry stock tank moments before it rained. Later, as water tumbled out of a shallow arroyo to splash against the dam, those peppy insects dived into the flood like joyful kamikazes. Who knows why the mass suicide took place? I know it must be part of the birthing process, a statement of life itself.

The day after a puddle is born, that statement is made vividly by tracks in the mud: of horned larks, a coyote, rabbits. But the message really goes up the next night after the Creation when spadefoot toads crawl from the earth and raise their incredible mating racket. Suddenly pinkie-sized toadlets are crowding every square foot of water.

A spadefoot passes all its days underground until the moisture arrives. Then it scrambles to the surface, eager to procreate. After a swift and noisy orgy, millions of eggs are laid. Immediately the adults tunnel back down to their eternal hibernations. Meanwhile in the pond a vertiginous evolution from egg to adult takes place in eleven to fifteen days. Carnivorous tadpoles devour each other in order to reach maturity before the puddle evaporates. In the middle of the growth cycle you can dip your cupped hands into the water anywhere and scoop out a dozen pollywogs.

Coyotes feast on the tadpoles, as do hawks and other birds. Robber flies suck them dry. Snakes gobble them like Jujyfruits.

The tadpoles constantly gasp for air on the surface. Or perhaps they are eating mosquito larvae. One year there were so many adolescent spadefoots in my favorite pond that I could hear a burbling like beer foam prickling, caused by all their mouths constantly breaking the surface.

SPADEFOOT BABIES eat each other and graze for microorganisms in the muck and knock off mosquito larvae by the billions. Every stock pond is a supermarket full of special treats. Most prolific are mosquitoes, then come the fairy shrimp and the clam shrimp. Overnight, the water is teeming with these critters. The egg sacs of estivating fairy shrimp may have been waiting in the dust for years. But give them a shot of H_2O and you almost have to jump back out of the way to avoid being trampled in their rush to propagate.

Fairy shrimp and clam shrimp are invertebrates, crustaceans, brachiopods. Their appendages function as both mouths and gills: they eat and breathe through their feet. Their eggs are stored in a brood chamber whose walls are transformed into a protective capsule called an ephippium. When the shrimp molts, the capsule sinks to the bottom and lies dormant. If the pond evaporates, no harm done. The ephippium is impervious to drying or freezing. Wind often blows the egg sac miles to another location. The being inside simply snoozes along in suspended animation, waiting for a new puddle; its egg sac is the brachiopodal version of a transmigrating soul.

But mosquitoes are the real workhorses of the stock pond food chain. A clarion call goes out and immediately the water is reeling with their larvae. Soon after a pond is created I can sit on the dam and marvel at the insects taking flight. Usually it's a trompe l'oeil situation. Not a cloud in the sky, and no wind either: a day placid as milk in a glass. But raindrops are falling onto the surface of my pond. Correction: not raindrops; it's only mosquitoes being born, hundreds of bugs hatching off the surface every second.

From the start mosquito larvae abound, clinging upside down to the underside of the water's surface skin. Pretty soon they pupate. But they are transparent and I cannot directly see them. However, sunlight reflected through their translucent bodies casts their shadows against the ooze a few inches below. One wriggles and then—*pop!*—it is gone . . . airborne . . .

. . . and instantly devoured.

THEY FALL VICTIM to a horde of minipredators, an aggressive Wild Bunch of hyperactive protein-scarfing machines. At twilight time my favorite hunters go to work.

Nighthawks are the most laconic snipers, openmouthed, systematically seining the air for food. Bats jitterbug back and forth, amazingly adroit with their echolocation techniques. Cliff swallows dart and dive gracefully. Their beaks just barely tweak the water—*tick!*—then the bird is away, leaving delicately expanding ripples in its wake.

The dam is honeycombed with kangaroo rat tunnels. Rabbits live among the gully rocks below. A modest prairie dog village is not far off: two of their tunnels are home to burrowing owls. With the advent of water, all these critters wake up and get active. Suddenly a marsh hawk appears, cruising low over the sage, scrounging for tidbits. Rattlesnakes naturally gravitate to the area. Water is like coffee, cocaine, crystal meth: it makes everything *alert*.

I SOON DISCOVER animal scat everywhere. Big blobs, little splashes, calciferous bird droppings—I inspect all of it with interest. Coyote scat is intriguing. I've seen it full of ants, piñon nutshells, apricot pits, mouse jawbones, lizard tails, and even small stones. Owl castings are apt to show up near the water as well.

One sweltering afternoon I stumbled upon the skull of a skunk. What was *it* doing way over there?

Lizards pop up from the rocks and dust. My favorites— the collared kind—run on their hind legs like toy dinosaurs. Obnoxious grasshoppers are all over the place, fluttering, crackling. I spot a shrike in a rabbitbrush bush. Wee spiders zip across lichen-covered rocks. Enormous tarantula hawks land in the slime and strut about busily. When a meadowlark warbles, I *listen*. Crickets strike up their monotonous concert at dusk.

How can such a small dab of water generate so much *noise*?

ONCE A YEAR I almost step on a rattlesnake at a stock pond. I park my truck and start walking towards the water. Inevitably a sixth sense impels me to glance down just as my left foot is landing two inches from a coiled serpent. For some reason I never scream or jump away. For some other reason the snake never rattles or strikes. Naturally, my heart always does a dive. When

I am past the snake I stop and turn around. I consider the dusky rattler and marvel. I respect and admire the danger. They create a landscape that declares, *Don't tread on me.*

Rattlesnakes: the mesa's testosterone.

KILLDEER PROVIDE the schmaltz. The baby ones, that is. Put water in a mesa stock tank and just watch the killdeer assemble. Their chicks are dandelion seed fluff balls walking on toothpick legs, positively adorable.

The most disturbing stockpond inhabitants are guajolotes.

A guajalote, in Nahuatl, is a turkey. A guajolote, in our local idiom, is the newt stage of the tiger salamander. They run rampant in northern New Mexico ditches and lakes and sewage plants. Nobody around here cottons to guajolotes. They are voracious predators. They're *ugly*. In past summers my kid and I caught them at Bernardin Lake and kept the beasts in an aquarium on the kitchen table. We fed them grasshoppers at lunch. That was cruel and fascinating "fun." Guajolotes demolish grasshoppers with brutal efficiency, striking like snakes and ingesting their victims accordingly.

But how do they wind up in a temporary stock pond out on the mesa? I have never solved this riddle.

VEGETATION CREATED by the magic wand of water includes wild sunflowers. And nettles on the dam. And profusions of gramma grass and ring muhly and western wheat grass. Also prickly buffalo burr, wild milkweed, Russian thistle, and even a few stalks of scarlet gilia. Winter fat flourishes, and rabbitbrush blossoms golden, exuding a skunklike odor.

Monarch butterflies are attracted by the milkweed. There are always hera moths and darning needles and dragonflies and honeybees. I recall a brief explosion of ladybugs. And I have found minuscule Day-Glo pink water mites shining in the mud.

In a wet season you can always count on hummingbirds. Seven years ago a billion cicadas were born. But I doubt water had much to do with them. They occupied every sage bush growing within ten square miles. The ground was pockmarked with their exit holes. They made a nonstop racket for two weeks, then disappeared.

IN GOOD YEARS a pond might hold water in September or October. If so, it becomes a powerful magnet to migrating birds. Mourning doves fly in at dusk and walk about on the damp shore, daintily sipping water. They are timid and blend with the landscape, almost invisible.

Avocets come specifically to fatten up. They are thin-legged birds with long upturned bills who work together in shallow water, three or four abreast, heads bowed and bills swinging back and forth like pendulums, stirring free the food with metronomic persistence. They rarely glance at me.

Once at a pond I flushed an ibis, a weird creature flapping off like a pterodactyl. I have jumped many small ducks: bufflehead, goldeneye, teal. If I sit down quickly and don't move, they'll fly in a circle around me once, twice, then set their wings and return to the water, gliding in a fluid line out of the sky down to a graceful landing.

Phalaropes appear also, nervously quartering the shrinking pond with bobbing heads, spinning in circles to stir up food. They never quit: back and forth, hither and yon, swimming... *swimming*. Like all other eating machines that abound in this sudden water, they are so full of energy. They *never* sit still.

One evening I found sharp little hoofprints near the water. The only explanation? There's been antelopes in the arroyo.

EVERYTHING FLOURISHES quickly at a stock pond, where all life is a race against time. Overnight the pollywogs lose their tails, crawl free of the water, disappear back into the earth. Each day the pond's surface area diminishes. The bats and nighthawks and swallows hunt faster. The guajolotes thrash about. Coyote paw prints at water's edge double and triple. Fairy shrimp and clam shrimp grow more frenetic in their zipping as the water races to dry up. Once there was a pond here; now there is a puddle. The skies stay blue, relentlessly azure. And the wind never rests for a minute.

Soon the puddle is no larger than my kitchen. The rains have ended; the sky remains desperately clear. Sunflowers dry up and wither. Grasses crackle underfoot. Mud splits open into chips and peels backward. Russian thistles become tumbleweeds. Wind blows ring muhly grass stems into a golden halo around the stock pond shore.

The wind sucks up the water, giving no mercy. The sun shines blindingly, killing every plant rising from the soil. There are no shadows to hide in. Dying now becomes an urgent business with the water drying up.

I want to cry, "Stop!" but I keep my mouth shut. Respect for nature is a commandment with me. What's "heartless" is uniquely human; what's impervious is strictly natural. I believe this death is wonderful.

Next thing you know, the swallows are gone. And no more bats, nighthawks, mourning doves, or killdeer. A duck wouldn't land in this fetid splash of goo, let alone an ibis. Dragonflies head for greener pastures.

I can still take a picture of clouds reflected in my postage stamp of water. . . but a day later it's over in the wink of an eye.

A sluggish guajolote tries to wedge itself into a damp crack in the bottom of the dry pond. But to no avail—the thing will die. Gnatlike bugs are flitting around its skin, preparing to feast. A nearby cluster of clam shrimp shells is glaring in the sun, all emptied out inside.

On the dam the nettles bake and turn brown. Wind erases footprints in dust the way it never could obliterate the tracks in mud. The grasshoppers are gone. So too the ladybugs and robber flies. I blinked and everything went to seed and only the sage remains. A landscape drab and dull, without fluttering beasts or cricket music at night. The air grows colder, sharp and dry.

Geese fly by overhead. . . and sandhill cranes. But there's no water anymore and nothing *but* water could call them down to earth.

In the end my stock ponds lie barren, empty, quiet. I visit a final time and sit on the dam as wind ruffles my hair. An entire universe has evaporated, a community disbanded and traveled elsewhere. I know seeds and fairy shrimp ephippiums lie in the dry dirt and thousands of toads are hibernating under the sage. But it's certainly a dreary landscape now that the water's gone.

I ENJOY the mesa in any incarnation. Yet what most gives my heart a lift is the startling intensity of aliveness when water gathers briefly in the desert.

Water is the one true power and glory that defines our universe of life. The heavens may twinkle with vast fires of exploding hydrogen, and the rocks on Jupiter may hold within their dark hearts the secrets to gravity and time, but—

But water gave rise to the only living web we'll ever know, and water created my active imagination. Consciousness and soul owe their incredible being to every drop of moisture that ever fell from a cloud and awakened a spadefoot toad, called forth a mosquito, or birthed a dragonfly.

HEAT

BRUCE BERGER

B orn and raised in suburban Chicago, poet and essayist Bruce Berger studied English at Yale before moving to Berkeley to attend the University of California. He has published poems in *Poetry* and *Orion* magazines, although he is best known for his suite of nature essays collected in *The Telling Distance* (1990), from which this selection is drawn, in which he examines the many facets of life presented by deserts. His other nonfiction works include *There Was a River* (1994), an account of a trip down the Colorado River before the completion of the Powell Dam; and *Almost an Island* (1998), about Baja California. His collected poems, *Facing the Music*, appeared in 1995 and won the Colorado Authors' League Award for Poetry. Berger now lives in Aspen, Colorado.

．　．　．

HEAT—UNLIKE COLD—IS ONE of those pleasures most keenly relished on the threshold of pain. It is oddly comforting to feel noon pouring down, to bake from beneath over bedrock, to find your marrow vaguely radiating. The best midsummer lunch is to gorge on enchiladas blazing with chiles, return to the car you have left in the sun with the windows rolled up, lock yourself in to steep in your own tears and sweat, then step out to find the heat wave has turned delicious. It is invigorating to walk over simmering gravel, feeling your soles come alive as they toughen, and baths are most relaxing when they resemble the first stages of missionary stew. Perhaps it is a desire to return to the womb, where we began for nine months at 98.6, that makes the warmth of alcohol so seductive, and one can comprehend— if not envy—the uncomforted who go through life sucking the eighty proof tit.

To test my heat tolerance I once went into the desert when daytime temperatures were easing off around 107 degrees, to see what might transpire. I expected an escort of insects, lizards, snakes, scorpions and chuckawallas, all the cold-blooded predators warmed like me for action, but the cactus stood in stunned silence. The afternoon lay like a ruin through which I seemed the only moving thing. My eyes ran with salt, my thirst became pathological, and I fled homeward to chug two beers nonstop before I could explain myself. But did I dream of cool mountains, as I did in childhood? No. It is as an adult, exiled to cool mountains, that I dream of the desert.

ACKNOWLEDGMENTS

"Port Etienne" excerpted from *Wind, Sand and Stars* by Antoine de Saint-Exupéry (New York: Reynal & Hitchcock, 1939).

"'Uweinat" excerpted from *Libyan Sands: Travel in a Dead World* by Ralph A. Bagnold (London: Michael Haag, 1935).

"The Camel of Cairo" excerpted from *A Social Departure: How Orthodocia and I Went Round the World* by Sara Jeannette Duncan (New York: D. Appleton and Company, 1890).

"The Caravan Meets with Disaster" excerpted from *My Life as an Explorer* by Sven Hedin (New York: Garden City Publishing Co. Inc., 1925).

"The Rumbling Sands" excerpted from *The Gobi Desert* by Mildred Cable and Francesca French (New York: The Macmillan Company, 1944).

"Jiayuguan" excerpted from *Behind the Wall: A Journey Through China,* by Colin Thubron (London: Heinemann, 1987).

"The Expedition to Eucla" excerpted from *Explorations in Australia* by John Forrest (London: Sampson, Low, Marston, Low & Searle, 1938).

"The Sand-Ribbed Desert" excerpted from *Australia's Empty Spaces* by Sidney Upton (London: George Allen & Unwin Ltd., 1938).

"The Atacama Desert" excerpted from *Bone and Dream: Into the World's Driest Desert* by Lake Sagaris. Copyright © 2000 by Lake Sagaris. Reprinted with permission of Knopf Canada.

"Antofagasta" excerpted from *Desert Memories: Journeys Through the Chilean North* by Ariel Dorfman. Copyright © 2004 by Ariel Dorfman. Reprinted with permission of The National Geographic Society (Washington: National Geographic Society, 2004).

"The Old Gringo Comes to Mexico to Die" excerpted from *The Old Gringo* by Carlos Fuentes, translated by Margaret Sayers Peden and the author (New York: Harper & Row Publishers, 1985).

"The Desert Smells Like Rain" excerpted from *The Desert Smells Like Rain: A Naturalist in Papago Indian Country* by Gary Paul Nabhan (San Francisco: North Point Press, 1982).

"Baja California" excerpted from *Eating Stone: Imagination and the Loss of the Wild* by Ellen Meloy. Copyright © 2005 by Mark Meloy. Used by permission of Pantheon Books, a division of Random House, Inc. (New York: Vintage Books, 2006).

"The Great American Desert" excerpted from *The Best of Edward Abbey*, edited and illustrated by Edward Abbey (San Francisco: Sierra Club Books, 1984).

"Shoshone Land" excerpted from *The Land of Little Rain* by Mary Austin (New York: Doubleday & Company Ltd., 1961).

"Steer Gulch" excerpted from *Wind in the Rock* by Ann Zwinger (New York: Harper & Row, 1978).

"The Raven" excerpted from *Desert Notes: Reflections in the Eye of a Raven* by Barry Holstun Lopez. Copyright © 1976 by Barry Lopez. Reprinted by permission of Sll/sterling Lord Literistic, Inc. (New York: Avon Books, 1981).

"Going Into the Desert" excerpted from *A Natural State: Essays on Texas* by Stephen Harrigan (Austin: University of Texas Press, 1988).

"The Holiness of Water" excerpted from *Dancing on the Stones: Selected Essays* by John Nichols. Copyright © 2000, University of New Mexico Press (Albuquerque: University of New Mexico Press, 2000).

"Heat" excerpted from *The Telling Distance: Conversations with the American Desert* by Bruce Berger (University of Arizona Press, 1991).

OTHER TITLES

The Sacred Balance: Rediscovering Our Place in Nature
by David Suzuki, Amanda McConnell,
and Adrienne Mason

An Enchantment of Birds by Richard Cannings

Where the Silence Rings by Wayne Grady, ed.

Dark Waters Dancing to a Breeze by Wayne Grady, ed.

Wisdom of the Elders by Peter Knudtson and David Suzuki

Rockies: A Natural History by Richard Cannings

Great Lakes by Wayne Grady

Wild Prairie by James R. Page

Prairie: A Natural History by Candace Savage

Tree by David Suzuki and Wayne Grady

The Sacred Balance: A Visual Celebration of Our Place in Nature
by David Suzuki and Amanda McConnell
with Maria DeCambra

From Naked Ape to Superspecies by David Suzuki and Holly Dressel

The David Suzuki Reader by David Suzuki

When the Wild Comes Leaping Up by David Suzuki, ed.

Good News for a Change by David Suzuki and Holly Dressel

The Last Great Sea by Terry Glavin

Northern Wild by David R. Boyd, ed.

Greenhouse by Gale E. Christianson

Vanishing Halo by Daniel Gawthrop

Dead Reckoning by Terry Glavin

Delgamuukw by Stan Persky

The Plundered Seas by Michael Berrill

DAVID SUZUKI FOUNDATION CHILDREN'S TITLES

There's a Barnyard in my Bedroom by David Suzuki;
illustrated by Eugenie Fernandes

Salmon Forest by David Suzuki and Sarah Ellis;
illustrated by Sheena Lott

You Are the Earth by David Suzuki and Kathy Vanderlinden

Eco-Fun by David Suzuki and Kathy Vanderlinden

The David Suzuki Foundation works through science and education to protect the diversity of nature and our quality of life, now and for the future.

With a goal of achieving sustainability within a generation, the Foundation collaborates with scientists, business and industry, academia, government and non-governmental organizations. We seek the best research to provide innovative solutions that will help build a clean, competitive economy that does not threaten the natural services that support all life.

The Foundation is a federally registered independent charity, which is supported with the help of over 50,000 individual donors across Canada and around the world.

We invite you to become a member. For more information on how you can support our work, please contact us:

THE DAVID SUZUKI FOUNDATION
219–2211 West 4th Avenue
Vancouver, BC, Canada V6K 4S2
www.davidsuzuki.org
contact@davidsuzuki.org
Tel: 604-732-4228 · Fax: 604-732-0752

Checks can be made payable to The David Suzuki Foundation. All donations are tax-deductible.
Canadian charitable registration: (BN) 12775 6716 rr0001
U.S. charitable registration: #94-3204049